What People Are Saying About

# Pagan Portals - Y Mabinogi

*Mhara Starling's Pagan Portals - Y Mabinogi* is the perfect introduction to the complex and beautiful stories foundational to Welsh mythology. Starling does a brilliant job of making the subject straightforward, even for people who may not have any previous knowledge of these tales, and she is honest about what we do and don't know about the material. Written in flowing prose that grabs the imagination as much as the stories themselves do; I highly recommend this for anyone interested in Welsh mythology, the Mabinogi, or Welsh culture.
**Morgan Daimler,** author of *Pagan Portals - Irish Paganism* and *Gods and Goddesses of Ireland*

In this beautiful introduction to the magical tapestry of the Mabinogi, Starling has succeeded in weaving together threads of mythology, enchantment, meaning, and deep, personal insights into a book that will open the doorway to a wondrous, mythical landscape. Written from the perspective of a person who has not only been raised and nurtured within these myths but also lived and breathed every aspect of them since her childhood. It is refreshing to read the words of a native person whose life is intricately woven into the beauty and magic of myth. In Starling's safe, capable, and experienced hands, the reader is in for a treat and insights that can only come from one who has lived the myths.
**Kristoffer Hughes,** Chief of the Anglesey Druid Order and author of *Cerridwen: Celtic Goddess of Ir Druidry*

Pagan Portals

# Y Mabinogi

Exploring the Magic and Wisdom of
Welsh Mythology

Pagan Portals
# Y Mabinogi

## Exploring the Magic and Wisdom of Welsh Mythology

Mhara Starling

MOON BOOKS

London, UK
Washington, DC, USA

First published by Moon Books, 2025
Moon Books is an imprint of Collective Ink Ltd.,
Unit 11, Shepperton House, 89 Shepperton Road, London, N1 3DF
office@collectiveinkbooks.com
www.collectiveinkbooks.com
www.moon-books.net

For distributor details and how to order please visit the 'Ordering' section on our website.

Text copyright: Mhara Starling 2024

ISBN: 978 1 80341 664 9
978 1 80341 870 4 (ebook)
Library of Congress Control Number: 2024937845

All rights reserved. Except for brief quotations in critical articles or reviews, no part of this book may be reproduced in any manner without prior written permission from the publishers.

The rights of Mhara Starling as author have been asserted in accordance with the Copyright, Designs and Patents Act 1988.

A CIP catalogue record for this book is available from the British Library.

Design: Lapiz Digital Services

UK: Printed and bound by CPI Group (UK) Ltd, Croydon, CR0 4YY
Printed in North America by CPI GPS partners

We operate a distinctive and ethical publishing philosophy in all areas of our business, from our global network of authors to production and worldwide distribution.

# Contents

| | |
|---|---|
| Introduction | 1 |
| The First Branch | 13 |
| The Second Branch | 29 |
| The Third Branch | 44 |
| The Fourth Branch | 56 |
| Beyond the Four Branches | 75 |
| A Guide to Welsh Pronunciation | 79 |
| Glossary of Names | 84 |
| Bibliography | 87 |

# Introduction

My first interaction with *Y Mabinogi* came about when I was very young. Having grown up in Wales, and in a predominately Welsh-speaking community at that, these stories were part of the very foundations of my youth. Long before I had ever read one of Grimm's tales, or the stories of Hans Christian Anderson, I was captivated by the magic of my own culture's lore.

At just six years old I helped in creating a huge art piece inspired by the four branches. At around eight years old I watched a small, local theatre company tell the story of Blodeuwedd, a woman who was cursed to become an owl. And at around ten years old I watched a flamboyant, funny, and musical pantomime production of the story of Branwen, a Welsh princess who married an Irish king.

These experiences influenced me in ways I never realised they would back then. It is funny to look back at these moments now and realise just how profound they were. Even considering the fact that in the small theatrical version of Blodeuwedd, they had the titular character burst into a heartfelt rendition of 'Breakaway' by Kelly Clarkson as she was transformed into an owl and flew away into the night sky. And the pantomime version of the story of Branwen featured a leather-clad, rough and ready, bearded version of the character known as Efnysien, who was portrayed as the story's primary villain. How they got away with dressing a man in essentially fetish wear for a children's performance is beyond me! But oh my, did all these experiences solidify me as a lover of mythology, and not just any mythology, Welsh mythology.

The stories found in *Y Mabinogi* are stories of giants, Otherworldly encounters, noble men and women, magicians, and enchantment. The very fantastical elements of these stories continue to inspire modern fantasy to this day. You cannot look at a shelf in the fantasy section of a bookshop without finding a book which has, in some way small or large, been influenced by these tales. And yet, beyond the rather enticing fantastical aspects of these stories, they persist because they speak to the very core of what it means to be human.

In this book we will explore what exactly *Y Mabinogi* is. Why are these stories often called the *four branches of the Mabinogi*? What is the difference between *Mabinogi* and *Mabinogion*? How old are the stories? And can we truly class them as 'mythology'? These are but some of the questions I hope to answer in this introduction to these enigmatic Welsh stories.

## The History of the *Mabinogi*

The stories we know today as the *Four Branches of the Mabinogi* made their way to us via medieval manuscripts. It is likely that these tales evolved from an oral tradition of storytelling, one that might stretch back through the mists of time. However, in the form that we know them today, with the characters we are fond of, and the escapades we enjoy reading of, they were preserved in glorious manuscripts. In particular, the majority of the stories can be found in two primary manuscripts.

The first is the *White Book of Rhydderch*. Known as Peniarth MS 4, and designated the title *Llyfr Gwyn Rhydderch*. The title of this book is likely a reference to the colour of its earlier binding (gwyn/white) as well as its early owner (Rhydderch). This manuscript is roughly dated to circa the 14th century. Within its pages are early examples of Welsh prose tales as well as poetry.

The second is the *Red Book of Hergest*. Known as Oxford Jesus College MS 111, and designated the title *Llyfr Coch Hergest*, named once again for the colour of its binding (coch/red), and the place where it once resided, Hergest Court in Herefordshire. Beyond more prose and poetry, this manuscript also contains herbal remedies and even entries on what might today be considered forms of folk magical healing attributed to the legendary Physicians of Myddfai. Dated again to circa the 14th or 15th centuries.

It is in these manuscripts that the majority of the stories that would become the emblematic tales of Wales were preserved. Fragments of the prose tales, and references to them can be found in other manuscripts from around the same period as well, but it is these two books which hold them in their most identifiable expression.

Whilst these manuscripts are roughly dated to sometime in the 14th or 15th centuries, dating the stories themselves is another thing entirely. Scholars continue to debate as to just how old the stories might be. Scholars of the late 19th and early 20th centuries, such as Welsh scholar Sir Ifor Williams, were under the belief that these stories extended back to around the 11th century (Charles-Edwards, 1996). Whilst recent scholarship tends to favour the notion that they are younger than that.

These debates as to a date, of course, focuses on them as literature, and not as stories which may have passed orally long before they were formally written down. The tales hold echoes of Celtic mythology which gives an indication that they probably had their origin in an oral tradition, as the stories likely long before they were preserved on paper were told or even performed, and even possibly changed over time (Davies, 2008).

Beyond the issue of date, there is also the mystery as to who exactly wrote them. The quest to find the 'author' of the tales is one that has become increasingly popular lately. Theories range from the idea that the stories were copied into manuscripts by monks operating from *Abaty Ystrad Fflur,* Strata Florida Abbey, Ceredigion (Charles-Edwards, 1996) all the way to the notion that there is evidence that the tales were likely written by a woman, as was proposed by Andrew Breeze who wrote *The Origins of the Four Branches of the Mabinogi* (Breeze, 2009). In fact, Breeze proposes the author may indeed be none other than

Gwenllian ferch Gruffudd, an infamous warrior princess from Welsh history. The truth is, we may never know who exactly the 'author' may have been.

The biggest question many have as to the origins of these stories, at least in modern Pagan circles, is whether they have an origin in the pre-Christian past. Whilst they are recognised today as medieval literature, the fact that they likely originated in an oral tradition of storytelling evokes imagery of the stories echoing an aspect of Welsh culture long before the coming of Christianity to these shores. Could the characters be the remnants of ancient deities? And the themes be a hint towards the myths, beliefs, and practices of Wales' pre-Christian Pagan ancestors?

Scholars such as Simon Rodway, who is also a lecturer of Celtic Studies at Aberystwyth University, have made clear that they are not entirely fond of the *Mabinogi* being referred to as 'Celtic Mythology'. Rodway wrote an essay titled *The Mabinogi and the Shadow of Celtic Mythology* for the journal *Studia Celtica* in 2018, which breaks down his views on the issues that arise when we shove the four branches into the box that is 'Celtic Mythology' (Rodway, 2018). The conclusion being that presenting the *Mabinogi* as 'Celtic Mythology' rather than simply 'Welsh Literature' is inappropriate, and often leads to the homogenisation of Welsh literature and culture into a watered down, homogenised Celtic fantasy. A fantasy which does not honour these tales for the brilliant works that they are, rooted not in some homogenous romanticised idea of 'Celtic' culture, but instead Welsh culture.

Whilst many scholars today may shy away from considering that the *Mabinogi* may teach us anything of Wales' pre-Christian past, the truth is we simply do not know how much of an influence ancient mythology may have had on the tales. It is generally accepted that these stories were part of the oral storytelling culture of Wales long before they were written down. However, the question of exactly how far into the past that oral storytelling might stretch is complex and near impossible to answer.

There are certainly hints towards pre-Christian beliefs and themes throughout the stories. For example, some character names are cognate with older pre-Christian deities. The most obvious being Mabon and Modron, who share a cognate name with Maponos and Matrona, deities associated with parts of Northern Britain and Gaul. Beyond this, there are also certain elements such as the Otherworld and the prevalence of shapeshifting and magic which likely hold an echo of a pre-Christian belief system (Hutton, 2023). Even Simon Rodway, who as we saw above, tends to disapprove of referring to the *Mabinogi* as 'Celtic Mythology' concedes that there are certainly fragments or echoes of older mythology present in these stories, however faint (Rodway, 2018).

One thing is certain, whilst these prose stories may hold countless mysteries that will undoubtedly be debated and discussed for many, many moons to come, they are now part and package of the cultural identity of Wales. We hold these stories as an emblem of our storytelling nature, and our fantastical perspective on life. They are not stories set *"Once upon a time, in a place far, far away..."* but instead stories that are rooted in locality and continue to inspire our culture and people. Beyond that, they have since expanded beyond the confines of Wales into the greater world.

Today, people from all over the planet turn to these stories to inspire, inform, and enchant. Scholars who adore digging into medieval history and literature, fiction authors who draw inspiration from the style and flow of the stories, and even modern-day Pagans who turn to these works as mythology to fuel their beliefs and practices.

I would say that there has not been a time when interest in *Y Mabinogi* was greater. Year after year new books, adaptations, artworks, and more seem to manifest themselves into reality, all on the topic of these Welsh stories. This fact warms my little Welsh heart to no end.

It is especially heartwarming when one considers that interest in *Y Mabinogi* outside of the Welsh speaking world only really began to pick up from the 18th century onwards. For the longest time these stories were seen as purely fanciful, yet fabulous stories worthless to anyone but children (Bromwich, 1996). Before the 18th century scholars tended to believe that the only worthwhile contribution the Welsh had to the world in the guise of literature were *Trioedd Ynys Prydein* (The Triads of the Island of Britain), a group of fragmented texts which preserve elements of Welsh lore and history. It was only with the rise of the romantic revival that interest in prose tales such as *Y Mabinogi* began to take hold.

The first person to ever make any strides in terms of translating *Y Mabinogi* was 18th century Welsh scholar William Owen Pughe (Bromwich, 1996). However, despite having translated the stories pretty much in their entirety, Pughe's clunky translations, lack of grammar skills, and the fact that he died not long after completing his manuscript meant that his work remained unpublished and barely made any waves, and his name is relatively unknown today.

Only three years after Pughe's death, a name which is likely more familiar released a translation which not only captured the essence of the original stories but also made them digestible and captivating for the lay reader. This was, of course, the translation by Lady Charlotte Guest, an English aristocrat and scholar. Being already learned in seven languages, Guest would eventually learn Welsh and turn her attention to translating various prose tales found in medieval Welsh manuscripts.

Lady Charlotte Guest's translation of the four branches and further prose and folk tales is still readily available today and is likely the version most are familiar with as it is accessible, and often free due to being in the public domain.

Since Guest's version, however, the four branches have been translated by various scholars and storytellers alike. They have been translated into various languages including French, German, and many more.

To this day new translations appear frequently, and beyond that adaptations, new interpretations, theatrical performances, songs, art, and more continues to be made based on *Y Mabinogi*. These stories grip us, and they continue to survive and thrive.

## *Mabinogi* vs *Mabinogion*, what's the difference?

One thing you may have already noticed is that these stories tend to be published under two different titles. When searching for a translation of these texts, you may come across both *Mabinogi* and *Mabinogion*. What is the difference between these two words? Is there a difference at all? And why do different translations choose one over the other?

The word *Mabinogi* appears in its middle Welsh spelling *Mabynnogy* at the close of each 'branch'. The stories are referred to as branches, a term used in both Welsh and French medieval literature, and is highly romantic, evoking imagery of a story which can be visualised as one great tree with many smaller branches taking us onto exciting new ventures. The term 'branches' or in Welsh, *Ceinciau,* is found in the medieval manuscripts also. At the end of each primary story, the text ends with the phrase...

*Ac Felly Terfyna'r Gainc Hon o'r Mabinogi*
(And thus ends this branch of the Mabinogi)

This small phrase, at the end of each story links all the stories together as a series which can be identified under the name *Mabinogi*. However, there is a variation of this word found in the medieval texts at the end of the first branch. Rather than *Mabynnogy*, the end of the first branch says *Mabynnogyon*, which in modern Welsh would be spelled *Mabinogion*.

For a while it was believed that *Mabinogion* was the plural form of *Mabinogi*. Under this impression, a single story or branch would be a *Mabinogi* and the collection of all four branches are the *Mabinogion*. However, there is an issue with this idea, and that issue is the fact that *Mabinogi* is already a plural word in the Welsh language.

Interestingly, it is believed that *Mabinogion* is in actuality a scribal error. You see, in the primary text before the phrase quoted above in the original manuscript, there is a sentence which ends with the word *Dyledogyon* (a word used to describe noble folk) and note this word has the same '*-yon*' at its end as the middle Welsh *Mabynnogyon*. These medieval manuscripts were written by hand, so it is fair to assume that sometimes the scribes may have been tired and made a few tiny mistakes. It is theorised that perhaps the scribe's eyes wandered and saw the word *Dyledogyon* whilst writing the word *Mabynnogy* and accidentally added an '*-on*' to the end (Ifans et al., 2007).

And therefore, technically, *Mabinogion* is nothing more than a scribal error. This is even more believable when one considers that every other time the word is used across the manuscripts it is always spelled *Mabinogi*. And so, the true title under which we can group the four branches is:

*Pedair Cainc y Mabinogi*
(The Four Branches of the *Mabinogi*)

And not the four branches of the *Mabinogion*. However, you may be wondering now, if this is the case, and most scholars accept that *Mabinogion* is nothing more than a scribal error, why is this word still used today as the title of various accurate, scholarly translations, articles, and works?

The simple answer to this question is that it has been around for so long that it has stuck! Many wrongfully attribute the word *Mabinogion* to Lady Charlotte Guest, as her translation of the stories were indeed published, and are still published under the title of *The Mabinogion*. Whilst it is true that Guest likely popularised the usage of the word, she was not the originator of using the word in this manner.

William Owen Pughe was the first to use this word as a catch-all for Welsh prose tales found in medieval manuscripts (Bromwich, 1996). He was also the first to put forth the idea that the word *Mabinogion* essentially meant 'Juvenalities' or 'Juvenile Romances'. Upholding the narrative that these were stories told primarily to children.

Lady Charlotte Guest's collection of translations of Welsh medieval literature included the four branches of the *Mabinogi*, but also other prose tales and the folk tale of the bard Taliesin's birth.

The term *Mabinogi* only truly applies to the four branches. There is no mention of this word, nor of the idea that the other prose tales found in the medieval manuscripts are at all related to the four branches outside of later translations. However, after Guest's translations proved popular, scholars from the 19th century onwards adopted the term *Mabinogion* as a catch-all term to group all Welsh prose tales found predominately in the *White Book of Rhydderch* and the *Red Book of Hergest*. And that tradition continues to this day.

In truth the term *Mabinogion* means nothing within a Welsh historical context beyond being a scribal error found once in the manuscripts. However, it has become a rather infamous word in the modern age. This term is known in Wales and beyond, and even modern-day Welsh translations of the stories will often use the word *Mabinogion* over *Mabinogi*. We have become accustomed to using it, and there is no other simple, succinct way of grouping the four branches and the other prose tales together. It works, and therefore it has stuck.

It is likely many choose to publish their translations under the term *Mabinogion*, as well as use the word over *Mabinogi* in various works because *Mabinogion* is more internationally identifiable. Whilst many Welsh language books tend to prefer *Mabinogi* in my experience, *Mabinogion* is a title that is now part of the global consciousness. As such, it just makes sense to continue using this word for ease.

A common misconception is that all of Welsh myth and lore can be grouped under the word *Mabinogion*. In recent years I have seen folks use this word when just discussing Welsh mythology and folklore in general. For example, it was only recently that I came across someone referring to the folk legend of *Llyn y Fan Fach*, a fairy story from the South of Wales, as being "a story from the *Mabinogion*", which it is not. It is important to acknowledge that just because a myth, legend, or folk tale is Welsh does not necessarily mean it is a *Mabinogi* story.

The stories which would be considered the *Mabinogi* "proper" are simply the four branches. Often identified under the titles of:

1. *Pwyll Pendefig Dyfed* (Pwyll, Prince of Dyfed)
2. *Branwen ferch Llŷr* (Branwen, Daughter of Llŷr)
3. *Manawydan fab Llŷr* (Manawydan, Son of Llŷr)
4. *Math fab Mathonwy* (Math, Son of Mathonwy)

Whereas the stories which are linked by modern scholars under the title *Mabinogion* usually include the four branches above, but also:

- *Breuddwyd Macsen Wledig* (The Dream of Maxen Wledig)
- *Lludd a Llefelys* (Lludd and Llefelys)
- *Culhwch ac Olwen* (Culhwch and Olwen)
- *Breuddwyd Rhonabwy* (The Dream of Rhonabwy)
- *Iarlles y Ffynnon / Owain* (The Lady of the Fountain / Owain)
- *Peredur fab Efrog* (Peredur, son of York)
- *Geraint fab Erbin* (Geraint, son of Erbin)

Introduction

And sometimes we see the story of *Ystoria Taliesin* (The Story/ History of Taliesin) included in the mix. Taliesin's story is somewhat of a wild card to include in compilations of the *Mabinogion*, firstly because it is a much later tale and is not found in the same manuscripts as the other stories mentioned, but also because this story is classed as a 'folk tale' as opposed to medieval prose. Nonetheless, Lady Charlotte Guest included it in her translations, and as such it has subsequently appeared in a few translations which followed.

This book will be focusing predominately on *Y Mabinogi*, as the title suggests, which are, of course, the four branches of the *Mabinogi* or the *Mabinogi* "proper" if you will. However, we will touch very briefly on the other prose tales as well at the close of the book.

## How to Use This Book

The primary purpose of this book is to act as a sort of 'Guidebook' for the curious Pagan, or as a stepping stone for those who wish to delve deeper into the *Mabinogi* but do not know where to start. What this book is not is a translation of the tales themselves. You can purchase many different translations of the tales today by brilliant translators and editors. My advice would be to pick up a good translation of the texts, read the stories thoroughly, and then read this book alongside them to gain further context.

My personal favourite current translation is the Sioned Davies translation published by Oxford University Press. However, my advice would be to try and get your hands on two or three different translations to compare and contrast the different ways translators have presented the tales into English.

I am no scholar, and therefore another thing this book is not is an academic investigation into these tales. Whilst I turn to academia to influence and inform my views of the tales, first and foremost I am simply a Pagan and Polytheist. This means that occasionally I will discuss how we, as modern pagans, might draw inspiration from these tales for our modern-day beliefs and practices.

My hope is that you will read this book and it will inspire you to delve deeper into the stories of my culture. That you will form emotional, visceral relationships with the characters presented in these texts. And, above all else, that you will want to learn more.

In the back of the book, I have included a guide to Welsh pronunciation, and a glossary of some of the names covered. Whilst reading, if you find yourself stuck on the pronunciations, simply glance over to that guide which will, I hope, offer clarity.

# The First Branch

We begin our journey in the South-West of Wales, in a place known as Dyfed. Today, Dyfed would be recognised in modern Wales as the Pembrokeshire area. This branch introduces us to Pwyll, a prince of Dyfed, Arawn, a King of the Otherworld or *Annwfn*, Hafgan, another King from the Otherworld who battles with Hafgan every year, Rhiannon, an Otherworldly maiden with divine qualities who marries Pwyll, and more.

The first branch deals with themes of communication and interaction with the Otherworld, sovereignty and marriage, princes and Kings, false accusations, and bereaved mothers. However, beyond all this there is seemingly a focus on being human, and the conditions we deal with as humans. Anxiety, caution, wisdom, recklessness, love, and friendship all play a role in the narrative woven.

These very human themes may, indeed, be the reason the stories of the four branches have survived as long as they have. Despite being set in a distant past, and preserved in medieval manuscripts with an obvious layering of medieval culture, even we today can relate to the development of the characters and the episodes they experience.

## Liminality & the Otherworld

A theme woven throughout the first branch, which may not be immediately apparent on a cursory read, is that of liminality. The scholar, Patrick Ford, discusses this in depth in his *Prolegomena to a Reading of the Mabinogi* (Ford, 1981). When we look at the various plot points throughout the first branch, it is made clear that many of the events are surrounded by motifs hinting towards a state of liminality.

From the very beginning of the tale, Pwyll is called, as though by intuition or destiny, to leave his chief court at Arberth and to embark upon a journey out into the wilds to go hunting. When he leaves his court, it is nighttime, the boundary between one day and the next. When morning comes, and he sets out to hunt, he is then thrust into a liminal state of existence, separated from his hunting companions, he is lost.

Interestingly, the place of which this hunt takes place is also one that exists in a liminal state of being. The text makes clear that Pwyll arrives at an area known as Glyn Cuch. Glyn Cuch today sits on the border between Pembrokeshire and Carmarthenshire. The Afon Teifi (the River Teifi) runs through this area, and it is an area that has historically been seen as a boundary between territories (Shack, 2015).

It is in this liminal state of being lost, and at this liminal place, Glyn Cuch, that Pwyll first encounters the Otherworld. He happens upon a pack of strange dogs, gleaming white is their fur, aside from on their ears, which are blood red. After a beat, he shoos the dogs away and sends his own dogs to feast on a stag which the unearthly white hounds had felled. As he does this, a mysterious figure clad in grey clothing, riding upon a great dapple-grey horse, with a hunting horn around his neck appears out of the thicket.

The rider claims that Pwyll has deeply offended him by shooing his hounds and sending his own dogs to feed upon the stag. Initially, Pwyll attempts to use his status as a Prince of Dyfed to calm the situation, but this grey figure cuts him off, telling him that he outranks Pwyll in status. He is Arawn, a King, and not just any King, a King of Annwfn.

Pwyll's blood runs cold as he hears this. Annwfn, the Otherworld, a strange yet powerful place. And here before him is a King from that mysterious land, and Pwyll has offended him.

This is our first encounter with the Otherworld in this tale, and it is all framed with this idea of liminality. This notion that the Otherworld makes itself apparent to those who find themselves in liminal states can also be found in later collections of folklore, seemingly expressing a folk belief present within the Welsh cultural continuum that the realm of the 'Other' and liminality are deeply connected.

Take, for example, the tale titled under *Owen Goes A-Wooing* in W. Jenkyn Thomas' popular collection of Welsh fairy stories *The Welsh Fairy Book*. In this tale Owen, a servant at a mansion in North Wales, is one night journeying to see his sweetheart who lives in a nearby village. On this very dark night, as he wanders near a great lake, he finds himself lost, and ultimately falls into the lake itself which acts as a portal between our world and the Otherworld. Owen finds himself in a new world, and, like Pwyll, comes across a denizen of this strange place (Thomas, 1907).

Tales like this one can be found throughout Welsh lore, recounting how folks often stumbled upon the Otherworld when lost, travelling at night, or traversing terrain which exist on a boundary or border — especially at the banks of rivers, or at the shores of lakes. They carry a similarity to Pwyll's encounter with Arawn. Liminality is often used as a literary motif within Welsh tradition to signify that the Otherworld is near.

The events of the first branch also seem to occur near a particular date, May Eve. This is the only date ever mentioned in the text itself, and we know that the majority of the events happen in one-year intervals. When Pwyll agrees to battle with Arawn's enemy, Hafgan, whilst under an enchantment which allows him to take on the form of Arawn, the battle is set to happen a year from the day Pwyll and Arawn met. When Pwyll eventually meets Rhiannon, and she makes clear her intentions to marry him, she arranges that they meet a year from their initial encounter. These one-year intervals occur over and over again, and yet the only accurate date we are given throughout the tale is May Eve.

We are told that every May Eve, a man named Teyrnon's mare gives birth to a foal, and every single year that foal would vanish. It is made clear in the tale that the loss of Rhiannon and Pwyll's son occurs at the same time as when this foal is snatched.

The significance of May Eve is interesting, as this date has long been a notable event in the Welsh folk calendar. In the Welsh language, May Eve is known as Nos Galan Mai. Galan is a mutation of the word Calan which translates to essentially mean "the first day of" or, to be more precise, the "calends" of. Nos means night or eve, and Mai is May in Welsh. So, Nos Galan Mai is the Eve of the Calends of May.

In the Welsh folk calendar Nos Galan Mai and May Day itself, Calan Mai, are considered particularly significant days. Their winter equivalents are Nos Galan Gaeaf and Calan Gaeaf, the eve of and the first day of winter. These times of year were not only times of celebration as folks honoured the turn of the seasons, as they marked the liminal period between the dark and light half of the year, but they were also said to hold rather magical qualities. It was at these times of year that the boundaries which might keep our world and the Otherworld somewhat separate were at their weakest. You were most likely to interact with the spirits of the dead, the land, and the Otherworld at these dates.

And so, once again, we have yet another link to liminality in the first branch. The events seem to coalesce at the liminal period that is Calan Mai, a time when the Welsh have long honoured the transition into the lighter and warmer part of the year, summer's beginning.

Via these themes of liminality, the characters of the first branch (and, as we will discover, the later branches also) interact with the looming force that is the Otherworld. Let us now turn our attention to the Otherworld of Welsh lore. What better place to start than with the name we give to this enchanting place.

Annwfn

(Ann-OO-vn)

In the Welsh language *An* can be used as an intensifying prefix. The second part of the word *nwfn* comes from the word dwfn, a word that is likely familiar to most Welsh speakers today. Dwfn essentially means 'deep' or 'depth'. Looking at it from this perspective, one theory as to the meaning of Annwfn is that it essentially means "The Very Deep".

A note: You might see the Otherworld referred to with two different spellings. Annwfn, and Annwn. Both of these spellings are correct, with Annwn being the most commonly used both in modern Welsh literature and vernacular. Annwfn is an older spelling, more in keeping with what is found in older manuscripts (Rudiger, 2022). I prefer to use the older spelling of Annwfn as it lends itself to showcasing that connotation of depth with the suffix of '-*nwfn*' originating in the word *dwfn* meaning deep. For consistency I will be using the Annwfn spelling throughout this book.

The definition of the Otherworld as being the place of depth makes sense on various levels. On one hand, the Otherworld is often described in Welsh lore as being a chthonic or underground realm. A place located directly beneath our world. Take, for example, the 12th century story of a boy who spent a period of time living among fairies.

According to Giraldus Cambrensis' *Itinerarium Cambriae* (The Itinerary Through Wales) the author, whilst travelling around Wales, once met a priest named Elidorus who had spent a significant period of his youth living with the fair folk. The story details how the realm of fairies is accessible via entryways in the Earth itself. Elidorus journeyed to this Otherworldly realm via an opening at the bank of a river near today's Swansea.

The Otherworld in this story is described as being a beautiful sub-terranean world. Meadows stretch as far as the eye can see, rivers wind their way across the landscape, and the place feels as though it is in a constant misty twilight, due to the lack of sunlight. The sky is the crust of Earth itself.

By this description, this Otherworld is literally a "deep place". A place located in the depths of the Earth itself. Whilst the name Annwfn does not appear in the original telling of this story in the 12th century Latin manuscript, later folk tales which would employ the name Annwfn to describe the Otherworld followed in a similar description of how the Otherworld looks and is accessed. A place deep below our own world, accessible via deep lakes, caves, and openings in the Earth.

In poetry and folk tales, the Otherworld is also described as being a place accessible via the sea, or even sometimes a place located beneath the sea. For example, in the 14th century poem *Preiddeu Annwn* (The Spoils of Annwfn) King Arthur and his retinue journey into the Otherworld via the sea. Another poem *Angar Kyfundawt* from the book of Taliesin describes Annwfn as being "below the Earth" (Haycock, 2007).

In this sense Annwfn is quite literally a place that is "very deep". A sub-terranean realm, or a realm found across the deep seas, or even sometimes under the sea itself. However, one could also argue that Annwfn can also metaphorically be seen as a place of depth.

In the Bardic tradition, Annwfn was considered the birthplace of Awen. In the aforementioned Taliesin poem *Angar Kyfundawt*, we see references made to this idea.

*Yn Annwfyn y diwyth,*
*Yn Annwfyn y gorwyth,*
*Yn Annwfyn is eluyd,*
*Yn awyr uch eluyd.*
(Haycock, 2007)

(In Annwfn the divisions of inspiration were ranged by divine hands,
In Annwfn they were formed,
In Annwfn beneath our world,

In the air above our world)
(My Translation)

This poem, and other poems found throughout Welsh history, paints us a picture of Awen as being a force of divinely touched inspiration, which, like a gentle breeze or like a river that flows, makes its way from the Otherworld into our own world. Here, Awen takes hold of us, and once it has its hold on us, we are moved to create, to inspire, to make form of that force.

To the bards, Annwfn, the Otherworld, became the birthplace of inspiration. A liminal, otherworldly place which aided in inspiring their powerful, moving words. They would connect to, and feel an affinity with the flow of Awen, and in turn were connecting with the Otherworld.

Awen, an Otherworldly force, aided the bard in delving into the very depths of their own soul in order to bring forth powerful, evocative poetry that sang with the magic of the Otherworld. Essentially, the bards were able to connect to such a force by delving into the depths of their being. Once again, we see this association between depth and Annwfn.

In later folklore Annwfn became the realm of what we might call today fairies. In Welsh, the native term used for these Otherworldly entities is primarily Y Tylwyth Teg. And I invite you to cast out any imagery of twee, small, human-like beings with gossamer wings and donning skirts made of flower petals when you envision the fairies of Welsh lore.

Throughout legend and lore, the fair folk are described primarily as being not too dissimilar to humans. Often the only thing that signifies that they are 'other' is their clothing, their ethereal beauty, or their magical abilities. Sometimes in certain stories from Welsh lore fairies are depicted as shorter than the average human (though no shorter than a child). However, for the most part, it is difficult to distinguish a fairy from an ordinary mortal, beyond certain signs and mannerisms.

The way the denizens of Annwfn are portrayed in later folklore is not entirely different to how they are portrayed here in the first branch either. In the *Mabinogi* the denizens of the Otherworld are never referred to as Tylwyth Teg, or by any other term which we might recognise as meaning 'fairies', and yet it would be incredibly difficult to distinguish between these Otherworldly folk and the fairy folk of later folklore. Here, they are also portrayed as looking no different to ordinary mortals, though being dressed in opulent, grand gowns of golden brocaded silk. They live in a world not unlike our own, but grander and more beautiful.

The description of Annwfn as a place not too dissimilar to our own world whilst having certain traits, such as being exceedingly more beautiful, or filled with riches, is also comparable to the realm from which the fair folk originate or dwell in later tales found in collections of folklore.

In Welsh lore there is no clear separation between our world and the Otherworld. No portal to pass through, no dense veil blocking our world and the Other. Our world and Annwfn is instead deeply connected in intimate ways, and often fairly accessible, if you know where to look or if you have a guide to usher you from one place to the next.

This is true for both the *Mabinogi*, and for folklore in general. In this first branch Pwyll is escorted to Annwfn by Arawn. There is no fanfare or theatrics to their journey into the Otherworld, instead they simply walk to Annwfn, side by side. In certain folk tales people are seen to accidentally slip through into Annwfn, as was mentioned earlier, in the story of Owen falling into Annwfn via a lake. Bodies of water, sub-terranean entryways, and liminal spaces in general seem to act as a boundary between our world and the Other.

The Otherworld is a deepening of our own world. A mirror image of our own existence. In this branch of the *Mabinogi* it is easy to deduce, especially considering that Arawn mentions

Hafgan, a King whose territory sits next to his and they often battle, that Annwfn is one singular realm divided into numerous Kingdoms. This is exactly how Wales has existed throughout history. The Otherworld is a realm of plenty, of abundance and opulence, of beauty and grace, of life and vitality. It is not an 'Underworld' where the dead are sent, but instead a vibrant realm of magic and adventure.

## Rhiannon & Sovereignty

Rhiannon is known across the world today as a highly popular Goddess among Neo-Pagan circles. A quick search online, or a flick through books which delve into modern Paganism and Witchcraft will draw up numerous descriptions of who exactly Rhiannon is. A Celtic Goddess associated with the moon, horses, magic, and divine femininity. But is this truly who Rhiannon is?

Rhiannon's origins lie here, in Welsh mythology. She is one of the most interesting characters in the *Mabinogi*, and what we will discover as we traverse up the tree and explore all four branches is that she has quite a prominent role. She is introduced to us here, in the very first branch.

After his time in Annwfn, Pwyll returned to his life as Prince of Dyfed. One day he voiced his desire to venture up to Gorsedd Arberth, a mound located at one of his chief courts. He was warned that according to known lore, a nobleman cannot sit atop Gorsedd Arberth without one of two things happening.

Either he would be badly injured, or even worse mortally wounded. Or, alternatively, he would see something wonderful. Pwyll had no fear, and so he journeyed to the mound with a selection of his men. There, atop the mound, he saw something remarkable. As he looked down across the landscape, he saw a woman, the most beautiful woman he had ever laid eyes on, riding atop a tall, pale-white horse. The woman wore garments of the most exquisite golden brocaded silks. She looked ethereal, and elegant.

Pwyll, acknowledging that her presence was unusual, and that she likely carried a message for someone in his Kingdom, sent his men to ride towards her and find out what it is she wants. But no matter how quickly his men galloped towards her on horseback, they could not catch up to her. Some enchantment must have been in place, for despite the fastest horses and the greatest riders in Pwyll's court exerting themselves to catch up to her, they never could. And she never looked as though she was riding at more than a slow, regal, careful pace. The faster they rode, the further away she seemed.

This went on for a while, as man after man was sent after this woman by Pwyll. Eventually they gave up for the evening and set off back to the court to sleep. The next day Pwyll travelled back to the mound and waited. Again, the woman appeared. This time Pwyll decided to pursue her himself. He galloped as fast as his horse would allow, but she remained a fair distance away from him.

Eventually Pwyll grew tired of chasing her, and so he called out, "Fair maiden, please, for the sake of the one you love the most, stop! Wait for me!"

And with those words, the woman's horse stopped in its tracks, and she turned to face Pwyll.

After some questioning, Pwyll discovers that she is Rhiannon, daughter of the mighty Hyfaidd Hen, a great King. She has come to Dyfed to seek out Pwyll, in hopes that he might marry her. Pwyll agreed to the union and arranged to meet Rhiannon in one year's time at the court of Hyfaidd Hen in order to make wedding preparations.

From the moment we meet Rhiannon it is clear that she has a magical allure about her. She is dressed similarly to the denizens of Annwfn which Pwyll spent time with as he took Arawn's place. The tale makes great effort to make it clear to the audience that Rhiannon is dressed in garments of golden brocaded silk. Perhaps this, a call back to the way the people in

Arawn's court were dressed, acts as a hint that Rhiannon is not of our world, a divine or Otherworldly maiden.

A word that one will stumble upon often when reading about Rhiannon, whether in scholarly articles and books, or in modern Pagan resources, is *sovereignty*. You likely already know the common definition of sovereignty, a word which denotes supreme power or authority. However, in this context, sovereignty is instead a reference to a motif many who study the broader subject of Celtic literature and mythology acknowledge.

Sovereignty in this context refers to the idea that a King's right to rule, and as such his ability to rule well, is only legitimised by a female sovereignty figure. It is usually in the union between the King and the sovereignty figure or Goddess that the King is finally elevated to true power and authority over his people and the land the sovereignty figure represents (Doan, 1985).

One theme of the first branch we will explore later in this chapter is how Pwyll ascends from being a rash, careless man to a wise, prudent lord. However, it is important to acknowledge now, before we explore Pwyll's journey, that much of this development was brought forth by Rhiannon herself. Rhiannon appears before Pwyll, with the intention of asking for Pwyll's hand in marriage. She has already chosen him as her consort, and yet, Pwyll must prove himself capable and worthy before she will even speak to him.

The first challenge Pwyll has in terms of approaching Rhiannon is understanding the correct and appropriate way to reach out to her. He appears riding upon a horse, trotting along at a steady amble, and yet none of Pwyll's finest men can reach her. She is an enchanted being, able to outrun them without so much as breaking a sweat. In this moment Pwyll does not use his common sense, and instead employs more force and strength. It is only when he uses his words and asks her to stop that she finally pays attention to him.

The action of simply asking her to stop bears more fruit than the amount of energy and time they had wasted by simply attempting to chase her down. The moment Pwyll asks her to stop, Rhiannon instantly responds with a line that is difficult to read without a hint of smugness and a vision of a smirk, *"For the sake of your horse, you should have asked me that a while ago!"*

Rhiannon seems to embody a sense of authority, power, and cunning in all she does. It was her choice to marry Pwyll, she sought him out, and when Pwyll acts a fool and promises a strange man, who turns out to be Rhiannon's former betrothed Gwawl, anything he so desires so long as it is his to give, it is Rhiannon who concocts a plan to get the better of Gwawl.

It is through Rhiannon that Pwyll often learns important lessons as to how to become a better ruler. And yet, Rhiannon is more than just a floaty, gentle Goddess whose entire purpose is to elevate a man.

Once Gwawl is defeated, Pwyll and Rhiannon consummate their marriage, a representation of the Goddess of sovereignty forming a union with the lord of the realm and legitimising his right to rule. And yet, from here we are instantly taken to another problem. For if Pwyll is to truly govern the land, then he must provide an heir.

After many years of Rhiannon and Pwyll failing to provide an heir, and being scrutinised for it, a son is finally born. But almost as soon as the son is born, at three days old, he is stolen away. Rhiannon is wrongfully accused of a foul and sinister deed, not only killing her son, but consuming him. Women who were placed in charge of watching the child, in fear for their lives, slaughter a puppy and cover Rhiannon in its blood so as to frame her, in hopes that they will not be on the receiving end of any punishment.

Rhiannon is certain she did not kill her own son. In this moment, she could lash out in fury at the women, but instead she shows them compassion. She tells them that she understands

The First Branch

their desire to hide the truth out of fear and asks them to reveal what truly happened. But they refuse to speak. And so, Rhiannon faces punishment.

It is at this point, separated from her child and husband, when the sovereignty of the lord and lady of the land is put into question, that Rhiannon begins to deteriorate. Becoming nothing but a beast of burden, forced to carry people on her back like a horse, and recount the deed she supposedly carried out to all. Her divine status means nothing now, and all that could save her is the return of her son.

In another part of the kingdom, we are told that a man named Teyrnon has a mare who, every May Day, gives birth to a foal. And, every May Day, this foal vanishes. The mare is left bereaved and without her foal. There is a strange parallel between the foal and Rhiannon, yet another hint of Rhiannon's association with horses.

Rhiannon arrives at the beginning of the first branch riding upon a great, pale white horse. This horse has an enchanted quality of being able to travel faster than any other horse, without any effort whatsoever. When she is wrongfully accused of killing and eating her own child, her punishment is to act like a horse, carrying visitors to the area upon her back and confessing her crimes to them. And here again, we draw a parallel between the mare who has lost her foal, to the Queen who has lost her heir.

The equine associations loaded in Rhiannon's stories have led many scholars to draw parallels between her and the Gallo-Brittonic Goddess Epona. The divine Queen Mare worshipped in Gaul and even as far North as Britain. To learn more about this, I suggest reading Jhenah Telyndru's *Pagan Portals: Rhiannon*.

Rhiannon's lost child appears outside Teyrnon's stables and is raised by Teyrnon and his wife. When he first arrives, he is wrapped in golden brocaded silk. As he rapidly matures, Teyrnon and his wife acknowledge the resemblance he has to

Pwyll and realise who he is. They take him back to Pwyll and Rhiannon, and upon his arrival, Rhiannon names him by crying out *"Byddai gwared a'm Pryder"* (what a relief from my anxiety). He is named Pryderi, a word that denotes anxiety.

With Pryderi's return, sovereignty is once again granted to Pwyll, and his domain prospers.

Within modern Paganism we might look to Rhiannon as a Goddess of Sovereignty, the very embodiment of the spirit of Wales itself. She is that power which carries our culture, heritage, and is a guardian of our beautiful mythic landscape. She has no associations in Welsh lore with the moon, and so I am uncertain where this modern interpretation of her arises from.

On a personal level, Rhiannon has long been perceived, by me, as an embodiment of the song of my culture's tenacity and endurance in the face of hardship. Welsh culture has long been suppressed, and attempts to wipe out our culture, language, heritage, and identity persist to this day. Yet, despite it all, we are still here. Rhiannon embodies that spirit in this branch. She is cunning, clever, calculated, ethereal, and tenacious. When I see efforts made to preserve our culture and inspire new generations to keep the sovereignty of our nation alive and well, I cannot help but envision Rhiannon upon her horse. She is there when I hear Dafydd Iwan's song *Yma O Hyd*. She is resilient, and as such inspires resilience.

### Pwyll & Wisdom – From Rash to Wise Ruler

Pryderi, the son of Rhiannon and Pwyll, is often perceived by many to be the "main character", so to speak, of the four branches. He is the only character to feature in all four branches, and so adds a feel of seriality to the tale. He will be explored in more depth later in this book.

Because of this focus on Pryderi, the first branch is often considered to be a tale of his origins and birth. However, I would argue that there is a greater story at play here, one far more important than the birth of a character which does not happen until late into the branch. The narrative which I believe to be of more importance in the first branch is that of Pwyll's development.

From the offset of the first branch, Pwyll is shown to be a character who tends to lack prudence and wisdom. He throws himself into situations without much thought, he is careless and rash. When he discovers unearthly hounds feasting upon a stag his first thought is not to seek out other hunters, but to steal the stag for his own hounds. When he sees a maiden riding upon a horse, he sends men to chase her down rather than simply asking her to wait. As a strange man asks him for a favour at his engagement feast, he promises him that he shall give him anything he desires, so long as it is his to give, and as such almost loses Rhiannon when this stranger says that he wishes to marry her.

The fact he seems to lack much prudence and wisdom is incredibly interesting, when we consider his name. Pwyll. To a non-Welsh speaking reader or listener of this story, the name may seem like simply a traditional Welsh name. And it is true, people are indeed named Pwyll in Wales today. However, the word Pwyll is more than just a name. Pwyll is a word that denotes caution, the careful consideration of a matter, common sense. To the Welsh speaking ear, we hear this word and the idea of taking great care or consideration is evoked.

This is a word commonly used in everyday Welsh speech today. I grew up hearing my mother or Grandmother shouting *"Cymera pwyll!"* when I was doing something that could potentially lead to danger or harm. They would use the word if I were climbing something steep and slippery, or running too quickly whilst on a busy street. It was their way of saying "Take care! Be careful! Use caution!".

Pwyll is defined in Welsh dictionaries today as essentially meaning consideration, care, prudence, or wisdom.

The first branch of the *Mabinogi* could effectively be read as Pwyll's journey to acquiring the wisdom, prudence, care needed to be a great lord of his realm. Or, in other words, his journey to achieving *Pwyll*.

Whilst the tale begins with Pwyll seemingly being a rash man often fumbling over situations he created for himself due to his lack of consideration and care, the story ends very differently. He is an accomplished and developed lord of Dyfed. His realm is now connected, deeply, with Arawn's, a relationship which brings abundance and treasures to him and his people. He has been chosen by Rhiannon, a figure who gifts Pwyll with the virtue of sovereignty, a fortuitous union which culminates in the birth of an heir, the expansion of his territory, and the love of his people.

We can learn much from delving into Pwyll's escapades and taking note of his journey to finding prudence and wisdom.

# The Second Branch

I believe the second branch is likely the branch I know most intimately out of all four. Not by my own choice, however. The second branch appears to be the most popular of all four branches on a mainstream level, schools seem to adore teaching it, theatre companies produce a stage adaptation of this branch frequently, and artists seem to be captivated by the visceral, intense imagery of it all.

On a personal level, I remember partaking in an art project where we created a large piece inspired by Brân's crossing of the sea over to Ireland when I was rather young. I saw pantomime productions of this branch, read it in class, and even produced my own stage production of it later in college (where I played Brân). Yes, it seems schools adore delving into the second branch. Which, on one hand is odd considering of all the branches this one is likely the most horrific!

The mutilation of horses, giants lured into iron huts to be gruesomely cooked to death, a giant woman who can give birth to full-grown, fully armed warriors. A child being thrown onto a fire and burning to death, a still animated severed head, the crushing of skulls, dead bodies flung into a cauldron to be reanimated into warrior zombies. This branch has all the hallmarks of an epic high-fantasy horror film. I am surprised no Hollywood producer has attempted to create a graphic, terrifying movie out of it yet.

On the other hand, this branch is likely the simplest in its core storyline. It would be difficult to summarise the entirety of any of the other branches in an easy to digest manner, as the narrative tends to meander in various directions. The second branch is rather simple to break down into its core elements, and beyond that it deals with themes that can easily translate into the modern world. Family dynamics, loyalty, abuse, honour, vengeance, and heartbreak are themes one will easily find here in the second branch or in any television soap opera today. Perhaps this is also why theatre companies, television producers, and schools choose to focus on this branch so much.

Let us begin our exploration of the second branch by first delving into the roles of certain characters.

## Brân the Blessed

The second branch opens by announcing to us that Brân is crowned King over the entirety of the Island of the Mighty, what we might refer to as Britain today. Brân is a giant, both in stature and in personality. He is the idealised King, portrayed as loyal, caring, wise, and in many ways divine.

After consideration and counsel, Brân agrees to give his sister Branwen in marriage to Matholwch, the Irish King, in a political union which will unite their two families and their two nations. With Ireland and The Island of the Mighty united, both will be inherently stronger. This union is, at least in theory, a wise decision. A decision which will benefit Brân's people and his land.

When Matholwch is insulted by Brân's half-brother, Efnysien, who feels as though he was insulted when Branwen was given to Matholwch without his permission, Brân attempts to reconcile the situation by offering the Irish King compensation. Later in the branch, when Brân is mortally wounded during the battle, his primary concern is ensuring the safety, and well-being of his men and his land. When eventually he dies, his head serves as a protective talisman, guarding his Island from threat.

His loyalty, compassion, and his care extend beyond his role as a King, but also to his role as a brother to Branwen. When Branwen eventually finds a way to let Brân know of the torment she is facing at the hands of her abusers, he is enraged. Matholwch has not only enacted cruelty upon his sister, but he sees this disrespect as an insult to himself. He swells with fury and passion, and he literally crosses the sea to avenge his sister. But not, of course, before appointing leaders to care for his land while he is away.

Brân's role as an ideal, competent, effective leader is echoed in many parts of Welsh culture today. When they arrive in Ireland to avenge Branwen and save her from the mistreatment she has endured, Matholwch's men retreat in fear across the River Liffey, a river filled with hurdles, with no bridge, and no way to sail over it. At this moment, Brân utters the infamous words:

*"A fo ben, bid bont"*
(He who is a leader, let him be a bridge)

At that moment he lays across the river, and acts as a bridge so that his men can cross the river and fight. The moment this happens, the Irish submit to defeat and offer to compensate Brân for the insult directed at him.

Those words *"A fo ben, bid bont"* have become a common proverb in Wales today. Uttered by political parties, used as a school motto, painted onto murals, and discussed in school settings. When Brân and his words are invoked today, it is usually a commentary on what true, good leadership is. Over the years I have heard many perceptions as to how we can interpret these wise words today. From the notion that a good leader must be ready to solve problems, as Brân did when faced with the obstacle of the river filled with hurdles, to the understanding that to be a good leader you must learn to effectively bridge many divides. I have also heard folks use this phrase as a means of saying that a true leader carries the weight of their people. That is to say that the privilege of leadership comes with a heavy responsibility.

Throughout this chapter so far, I have referred to the King of the Island of the Mighty as simply Brân. However, if you were to read a translation of the *Mabinogi* today you are more likely to know him as Bendigeidfran.

The name Bendigeidfran essentially denotes an epithet or title bestowed upon Brân. The name translates to mean Brân the Blessed. Brân is a word used to describe a Crow, or Raven, or even any black bird found in the Corvidae family, and so we could translate Bendigeidfran to literally mean 'The Blessed Crow/Raven". Brân is identified as being the son of Llŷr in the *Mabinogi*, as he is in earlier medieval Welsh poetry. In fact, the name Bendigeidfran, which in the manuscripts is expressed as *Brân Vendigeit*, is only found in the manuscripts which preserve the second branch. All other mentions of Brân outside of the *Mabinogi* texts simply refer to him as *Brân fab Llŷr*, Brân the son of Llŷr (Bromwich, 2014).

Llŷr is expressed in modern Pagan traditions today as a Welsh Sea God (Hughes, 2014). In the *Mabinogi* there are no specific stories which feature him, and yet his shadow looms over the four branches as they sometimes follow the lives of his children. Brân, Branwen, and Manawydan are all children of Llŷr. I believe the perception of Llŷr as a God of the seas is linked to the etymology of his name. The name Llŷr shares an etymological root with the Welsh word for 'to flow', which is *Llifo*. In ancient Welsh poetry we also see bards utilise the word Llŷr and Llyrion to describe the sea and seas (Bromwich, 2014). A Welsh genealogical tract *Bonedd y Saint* makes reference to a Llŷr Marini (Bromwich, 2014), a strange epithet which fuses Welsh and Latin words for the same thing! If Llŷr translates to mean "sea", and Marini comes from the Latin word to denote "seas" then this name translates to "The Sea of the Seas".

## Branwen

One of the three chief maidens, matriarchs, or ancestors of the Isle of the Mighty. When Branwen is given to Matholwch as a wife she is referred to as being such. The original word used here is *rhiain* a word rather difficult to fully translate. Sioned Davies' edition of the *Mabinogi* tends to favour the translation as being 'maiden' so that Branwen is one of the three chief maidens of the Island. Though, Davies does make clear in her explanatory notes that this word could also be translated to mean 'ancestors' (Davies, 2007). The Dafydd and Rhiannon Ifans version in the Welsh language refers to her as one of three "Prif Riant" of the Island (Ifans & Ifans, 2007). *Riant* is a mutation of *Rhiant* the Welsh word for 'parent' but also ancestor or elder.

This reference to a triad has long been the subject of discussion among Celtic scholars. Patrick Ford notes that W.J. Gryffudd associated the word *rhiain* with a possible link to words meaning 'queen', making Branwen one of the three Chief Queens, whereas Sir Ifor Williams went with the notion that it referred to her as a 'chief parent' or 'ancestress' (Ford, 1987). Regardless of the true translation or meaning, the fact she is described not only as the fairest maiden in all the world, but also as a chief parent, ancestress, queen, or matriarch bolsters her as incredibly important. A true match for the King of Ireland, and their union would bridge their two kins together. Who the other two 'Chief Matriarchs/Queens/Ancestresses' are is unknown, though Sir Ifor Williams believed it may have referred to Branwen, Rhiannon, and Arianrhod, the primary matriarchs of the four branches (Ford, 1987).

Branwen's name, at first glance, seems rather straightforward to any reader who understands the Welsh language. Bran, as we have already touched upon in the name of her brother, is the Welsh word for a corvid, usually a crow or raven. The second part of her name, Wen, is usually attributed as deriving from the word 'Gwyn' meaning 'white'. However, often when the word 'Gwyn'/'Wen' is translated from Welsh into English, the multi-faceted definition of this word isn't explored. Whilst yes, Gwyn means 'White' in Welsh, as in the colour white, it is also a word that denotes fairness, holiness, or the blessed nature of something. It can also be used to describe something that is shining, bright, or brilliant.

Whilst the common translation of Branwen's name as a 'white raven/crow' is not incorrect, it is not the only way we can look at her name. We could also translate it to mean Holy or Fair Raven/Crow/Corvid. The term Brân Wen (literally 'white crow') is also used in Welsh to describe something that is exceptionally rare. Branwen in this story is essentially described as a rarity also, as the fairest maiden in the world and the potential bridge between two peoples.

Rachel Bromwich details in *Trioedd Ynys Prydein* how she believes that Branwen's name was originally Bronwen (Bromwich, 2014). This spelling is used once in a manuscript which preserves this branch. Bromwich's notion is that the vowel in Bronwen changed from an 'o' to an 'a' in order to match her brother's name, Bendigeidfran/ Brân. The translation of the name Bronwen is 'fair/white breast'. The idea of a maiden being described as having a fair or white breast is common in Welsh prose, Olwen in *How Culhwch won Olwen* is one example referred to as having breasts whiter than the breast of a swan (Davies, 2007).

However, something I find rather intriguing is the fact that one could argue that Branwen and Bendigeidfran are the exact same name. Branwen can be translated to mean white, fair, holy, or even blessed crow. Bendigeidfran also means blessed crow. Patrick Ford notes this in his essay *Branwen: A Study of the Celtic Affinities* and goes a step further to propose that perhaps Branwen is the older, native form of the name. Bendigeidfran's name after all draws upon the word Bendigeid/Vendigeid, which evolved from the Latin Benedic. Whereas Branwen possibly developed natively (Ford, 1985).

Branwen shares a common thread with Rhiannon, in that they both suffered after their marriages. However, where one cannot help but admire Rhiannon's cunning, calculated, and resilient nature, it is hard to read of Branwen's plight without simply feeling a sense of pity and sorrow.

Branwen serves as a bridge between two kins, two nations, and yet she is seemingly looked upon as nothing more than a cog in a machine, a hurdle in a game. Her own independence, autonomy, and identity is overlooked in favour of seeing her as nothing more than a political tool. Matholwch gives in to the pressures placed upon him by his people and sends her to the kitchens where she is abused daily.

Unlike Rhiannon, who solved some of the issues in the first branch via her cunning nature and magical resources, Branwen is no Otherworldly sorceress. She is merely a foreigner in a strange land, an intruder on an unfamiliar culture, living among folk who will never accept her as their own, despite the efforts she makes to fit in and perform her duties. She has no magical bag or power that will get her out of the mess she has found herself in, and so she turns to the one thing she does have: Hope.

The one thing she is able to do is befriend a small, fledgling bird. She communes with a starling, and trains it over a period of three years. Hoping, that against all odds, this bird will manage to fly across the waters back to Wales and send a message to Branwen's family of her plight. And if successful, Brân will come and rescue her. Hope is her only chance at this point, it is all she has to live for.

Brân receives the message and comes to her rescue. He wades across the waters which divide Wales and Ireland, and as a giant he did this with ease. The Irish men upon seeing him believe his head to be a great mountain on a previously unseen island, and the ships around him to be a forest. They seek Branwen's help to decipher what this strange island is, and Branwen says to them plainly "My brother is here, and he is angry".

Eventually the events of the story culminate in a great war, where the vast majority die. Branwen survives the terrors of the battle, but her son does not, her brother is dying, her half-brother also gone, and both Ireland and the Island of the Mighty have been ravaged by the fighting.

Branwen carries all the shame and guilt of this war, internalising it all and blaming no one but herself. As she returns back to Wales, landing on Anglesey, she stands at Aber Alaw, looking over to both Ireland in the distance and Wales before her. She cannot bare all the destruction, and all the guilt she has internalised. With that, she lets out an almighty sigh, and dies of a broken heart.

In a field not far from the Afon Alaw on Anglesey sits a Bronze Age funerary mound. This mound is called *Bedd Branwen* — the grave or tomb of Branwen. Whilst the mound itself is in actuality an ancient monument, the burial site that likely belonged to a Bronze Age family, this site has been linked to the story of Branwen for at least two centuries now. In the early 19th century excavations of the mound revealed a buried urn with bones inside (Lynch, 1970). Many believed these bones belonged to a woman, and therefore conclusions were drawn that the remains of Branwen had been found. The fact folks on Anglesey truly believe Bedd Branwen to be the true tomb of Branwen is not too far-fetched, considering after her death in the original text it is said the survivors who journeyed back to Wales with her created a four-sided grave and laid her to rest at the banks of the Afon Alaw. The Bronze Age mound has a boulder or standing stone at its centre, split in two, it stands almost like a tombstone. It is not difficult to see how conclusions were drawn.

Regardless of whether this is or is not the true tomb of Branwen, it has become such within folk belief and tradition. To this day people will journey to this ancient monument and leave flowers for Branwen atop the stone. People will take their children and tell them the story of the Welsh princess who died here. Local lore even states that starlings come at certain times of the year and dance in their murmurations above the banks of the Alaw. Descendants of the starling that Branwen sought the aid of dance through the skies in memory of her.

## The Cauldron

Throughout Welsh lore, there are two primary tools used by those who weave magic. The first is the wand, the tool of the magician, which we will discuss in more depth when delving into the fourth branch. The other is the cauldron. Possibly one of the most emblematic symbols associated with Witchcraft today, the cauldron features heavily in both Irish and Welsh medieval literature (Joy, 2014). Beyond playing a role in myth and lore, the cauldron has long been an important vessel used by people for thousands of years. Archaeologists find cauldrons across most of Northwestern Europe, and of course, that includes here in Wales.

Beyond being simply a cooking utensil, the cauldron was the heart of the community. I can only imagine the stories, the songs, the joys, the trials and tribulations, the laughter and the tears a communal cauldron might have been witness to during Iron Age Britain. I mention the Iron Age because several archaeological excavations have found cauldrons dating to that period across Wales. Interestingly, many cauldrons seem to have been flung into bodies of water, perhaps as offerings in ritualistic practice. An example would be some of the cauldrons on display at the National Museum, Cardiff. Included in their collections are fragments of cauldrons pulled out of Llyn Cerrig Bach, a lake on Anglesey where a hoard of Iron Age items had been discovered.

One of the better-known cauldrons of Welsh lore is likely the cauldron which belonged to the Witch, Cerridwen, who brewed a potion of Awen in order to better her son who was afflicted with utter hideousness. And yet, it is the cauldron found in the second branch of the *Mabinogi* which has likely impacted global mainstream pop culture the most.

The cauldron in this branch is referred to as the *Pair Dadeni*, the Cauldron of Rebirth. It has a magical property in that if you are to throw a slain warrior into it, the warrior shall rise from the dead, albeit without the power of speech. It is this magical property attributed to the cauldron that has gripped the imagination over the last century. In the 1960's Lloyd Alexander wrote a series of children's high fantasy books, a pentalogy known under the collective title of *The Chronicles of Prydain*. The series in its entirety draws inspiration from Welsh mythology and lore. Character names from the *Mabinogi*, themes and storylines are all drawn from to create a fantastical world. The second book in the series is titled *The Black Cauldron* and features a magical cauldron owned by the Lord of Death, Arawn. In these books the cauldron is used to create an army of 'Cauldron-Born', undead mute warriors who serve the antagonist.

In 1985 Walt Disney Studios produced a feature length animated film based on the Lloyd Alexander books, under the title of the second book in *The Chronicles of Prydain* series, *The Black Cauldron*. This animated film is far from what one usually envisions when thinking of Disney films. The depiction of the dead warriors rising from the cauldron is rather unsettling and gruesome for a children's film. It is clear the cauldron, in both Lloyd Alexander's books and in the Walt Disney adaptation, drew inspiration heavily from the cauldron which Brân gifted to Matholwch. Whenever I speak of the second branch publicly or online, I always receive perplexed comments asking "wait, that sounds familiar, is that where the Black Cauldron got its inspiration from?", which shocks me, as I always believed it common knowledge.

One interesting thing about the *Pair Dadeni* is that the second branch offers us the lore as to how it came to be in Brân's possession. The cauldron was originally owned by two giants from Ireland. Matholwch had interacted with these giants long before he came to Wales to marry Branwen.

The Second Branch

Two giants rose out of a lake called 'The Lake of the Cauldron' in Ireland. The male giant was called Llasar Llaes Gyfnewid, he was described as hideously ugly and tremendously large. He carried the cauldron on his back. The female giant was named Cymidei Cymeinfoll, and she was twice the size of Llasar. Cymidei was pregnant, and she had a strange power. She could give birth to fully formed, fully armed warriors.

Matholwch took these giants in, and they lived among him and his people for years. All was well in the first year, but as time passed, they began to irritate the Irish people. They longed to be rid of them and eventually pressured Matholwch to find a way to get them out of their lives. They would not leave of their own free will, and Matholwch and his men were too afraid to try and drive them out by force, due to the fact they were skilled in battle and had children who were fierce warriors. And so, Matholwch's only solution is to attempt to murder them by luring them into a house made of iron and burning them alive. This plan fails, however, and the two giants escape the iron house and Ireland altogether. They sought refuge in Wales, where they gifted Brân with the cauldron. From there they populated many parts of Wales with the finest warriors who had the finest weapons.

The names of these giants who were keepers of the cauldron before Brân was are rather interesting. Cymidei Cymeinfoll's name translates to have associations with battle or war. Cymidei is likely associated with the word *cymid* which is literally 'battle'. Cymeinfoll is likely a fusion of two different words *Cymaint* meaning great or large quantity, and *boll* meaning distended or wide-open. The allusion in this name is that she is literally filled with a large quantity of battle. Or, to put it in more poetic speech, she is heavily pregnant with battle. A great descriptor of a giantess who births fully grown, fully formed, fully armed warriors.

Llasar Llaes Gyfnewid's name is a somewhat difficult to fully decipher. Ifor Williams believed that Llasar was related to the Irish word *lasar* meaning 'flame' (Williams, 1930). Llasar is, however, a Welsh word, which means azure, or a type of blue substance used to decorate shields. Both of these words would make sense in the context of a giant, I will explain why 'flame' would work in a moment, but a substance used to adorn shields has associations with battle, and as his wife, offspring, and his cauldron are associated with warriors it would only make sense that he would have a name that is battle oriented. Llaes is a word which means free or careless. Gyfnewid translates to mean change or trade.

And so, we have two possible name meanings here. Again, taking some poetic license here, his name could be translated to describe an ever-changing warrior. Or, alternatively, if we are to accept that Llasar is related to *lasar*, flame, then his name could be translated to mean "ever-changing flame".

Personally, I am fond of the flame theory. Llasar's wife Cymidei is almost a living embodiment of the cauldron that she and her husband are the keepers of. The cauldron has the power to revive dead warriors, whereas she creates fully formed warriors in her body. Her husband, who quite likely helps in the conception of said warriors could be compared to the flame beneath a cauldron. She is the vessel, he is the flame, and together they create exceptional, supernatural warriors. But perhaps that is too far-fetched of a notion for some.

## War and Strife

The second branch does a remarkable job of reflecting the terrors of war and turmoil. In the same manner that the first branch dealt with the ins and outs of courtly life and the life of nobles, this branch deals not only with Kings and nobles, but also with war and the warrior class. The story emphasises and animates the absolute horror that war can bring. And yet, there is another layer to this branch as well, for hidden underneath a story packed to the brim with giants, mystical cauldrons, helpful, friendly starlings, and severed heads that continue to speak ... are echoes of a complex legal system.

Medieval Wales had a strong legal culture that hinged on ideas of shame and reparation (Ford, 1987). The second branch is set amidst the backdrop of this legal system. Insult, shame, and honour sits as the core motivations behind many of the key components of this tale. What begins as a tale of unification takes a dark turn once certain characters feel that their honour has been tainted.

Efnysien, acting out of rage and fury mutilates Matholwch's horses, and he feels right in doing so because he believes that for Branwen to be married without his permission is an affront to his honour, an insult to his character and status. This act then causes Matholwch to feel insulted and as though his honour has been dinted. Compensation is paid to Matholwch as a means to restore his honour, but then another insult is thrown, this time towards both Branwen and Brân, when after accepting the compensation provided by Brân, Matholwch bows to the pressure of his people and mistreats Branwen. In response, Brân rains vengeance. The two clans go to war.

This entire narrative fits neatly into the concept of *sarhaed* rooted in the medieval Welsh legal system. *Sarhaed* essentially stands for the compensation paid to a person whom has suffered an act of intentional harm or shame (Owen, 1980). It is a form of reparation or apology for insult or dishonour caused. By delivering *sarhaed* the victim's honour is restored. The price of said compensation was determined based on the status of the victim. If *sarhaed* was not paid, then the victim could enact vengeance. Brân's offer of compensation in the form of horses, a large rod of silver, a plate of gold, and the cauldron of rebirth essentially acted as the *sarhaed* or insult price, to make amends and restore Matholwch's honour after his horses were mutilated.

At the heart of the second branch is the tale of the unification of two peoples, two clans, and how insult to one's honour can affect said unification in drastic and horrific ways. Ultimately, however, the second branch can also serve as a cautionary tale that vengeance often leads to nothing but senseless destruction. An interesting question to ask at this point is who, or what, was the cause of all the horrors of the second branch? Is any one character to blame? Branwen died of a broken heart, believing that all of this pain was brought about because of her. But who else might be at fault? The easiest way to answer this question is by, of course, turning our eyes onto Efnysien. He is certainly pinned as the "villain" of the narrative in many modern interpretations. However, what of Brân? The supposed "perfect leader"? Was he perhaps incorrect in giving Branwen to Matholwch? Was this choice done with as much thought and deliberation as it could have? I am not too keen on the desire many in modern Paganism have to label every single female character a "sovereignty Goddess". However, if we were to look at Branwen via that lens, could she be a representation of Wales' sovereignty? And Brân simply carted her off in favour of greater strength for his land? Or, what of Matholwch? Who scorned the compensation given by Brân and mistreated Branwen?

There are many places and characters we could lay the "blame" of the atrocities of the second branch. Ultimately, however, it was the constant seeking of vengeance which fanned the flames for such destruction.

## The Island of Gwales

The end of the second branch seems dim, and grey. Only eight survive the terrors of the war, and upon arriving home, Branwen dies too, leaving them at seven. Brân's severed head keeps the seven survivors' company, as they learn that the Isle of the Mighty has been overrun by Caswallon, son of Beli.

As they arrive at Harlech, they are lulled into a sense of security and peace by the Birds of Rhiannon, mystical birds whose song can be heard clearly even when they seem to be far out at sea. There they stay, soothed by bird song, for seven years. After this seven-year interlude, the seven survivors, now known as the Assembly of the Noble Head, spend eighty years on Gwales.

Gwales seems to have an Otherworldly quality to it. Located off the coast of Pembrokeshire, Grassholm Island has become associated with this mystical island. Upon this island they find a pleasant royal dwelling, and they stay here for decades, unafflicted by the pain, trauma, and grief they endured during the war. Entertained by Brân's severed head. Time also seems not to affect them, as they do not seem to age whilst here. Brân stays alive despite being detached from the rest of his body. Eventually a taboo is broken, and all the grief and pain they have not known rushes back to them, and Brân dies. In death his head is buried under the white hill in London, as a protective talisman, keeping the Isle of the Mighty safe from invaders and trouble. The white hill has been identified as the location where today you will find the Tower of London, and it is interesting that the tower still has associations with corvids today. Ravens dwell in the grounds of the tower, and as of when I am writing this book, one of the ravens is even called Branwen, according to the official tower of London website. Even more interesting is the fact that these ravens also seem to offer a sense of protection and security to the tower itself, for London lore states that should the ravens leave the tower, the tower will surely fall.

The Island of Gwales seems to carry certain motifs that we would later see in folklore associated with enchanted fairy islands. Pembrokeshire folklore is abundant with stories of these islands which appear, and disappear frequently (Jones, 1930). These islands are often home to fairy beings, and usually have associations with invisibility, temporal distortion, and a paradisical nature. Perhaps they are part of the same folk tradition of belief in mystical islands, or perhaps the islands of later folklore were inspired by the Island of Gwales.

# The Third Branch

After all the devastation, the story continues. The third branch continues directly from where we left off, in the aftermath of the battles in Ireland and the time spent on Gwales. The primary story of the third branch is that of the enchantment cast upon Dyfed, the location of the first branch. We once again return to familiar characters such as Rhiannon, and her son Pryderi.

There are many themes we could explore in the third branch, such as the theme of being a stranger in a strange land. When Dyfed is left deserted due to a magical mist, the four primary characters of this branch venture into England. There, they turn their attention to becoming skilled craftspeople. Learning to make saddles, shields, and shoes. These journeys into England, nestled between the enchantment and disenchantment of Manawydan's newly acquired domain, provide our characters with a chance to learn new skills, and develop themselves.

However, I believe the best place to start with the third branch is by looking at Manawydan himself.

### Manawydan – A Leader of Wisdom and Caution

The third branch focuses on Manawydan fab Llŷr, a character we were introduced to in the second branch. The brother of Brân and Branwen, Manawydan was one of the seven survivors to have journeyed to the Island of Gwales with Brân's severed head as it remained animated. He then ventured to the White Hill in London with his retinue, to bury his brother's head as a talisman of protection for the Island of the Mighty.

At the beginning of this branch Manawydan laments that he has nowhere to go, no home to return to. His brother, the former King of the Island is dead, as is his sister. His cousin Caswallon now sits on the throne, and yet he is only there due to trickery and murder. Manawydan has every right to

The Third Branch

challenge Caswallon's standing as King, and yet he chooses not to. Instead, he journeys to Dyfed with Pryderi, who has offered all seven cantrefs of Dyfed to him, and with that, a union with Rhiannon. Upon meeting Rhiannon, they get along well, and marry, making Manawydan the new Lord of Dyfed. He is Rhiannon's second consort, Pwyll is long dead.

Manawydan's name may help us understand him better. Rachel Bromwich in *Trioedd Ynys Prydein* draws a link between the name Manawydan and the territorial name *Manaw* which referred historically to the Isle of Man, but also to a region known as *Manaw Gododdin* (Bromwich, 2014). The region known as *Manaw Gododdin* was situated in what is referred to as *Yr Hen Ogledd* (The Old North) which we might know today as being certain areas in the southernmost part of Scotland and Northernmost part of England. In the early Middle Ages, these regions would have been occupied and ruled over by Brittonic-speaking people, people who spoke a language related to modern day Welsh. *Manaw Gododdin* in particular would have been located in what is today the county of Clackmannanshire. In fact, the *mannan* in *Clackmannanshire* as well as the town of *Clackmannan* derives from the Brythonic name *Manaw*.

This association with *Manaw* has led scholars to draw links between Manawydan and the Irish Manannán mac Lir. Manannán's name also has an etymological link with the Isle of Man, and in Irish lore he is also said to reside there. Manannán is the son of Lir, and Lir translates to mean 'sea', so therefore he is son of the Sea (Daimler, 2016). Manawydan is son of Llŷr, and as we explored in the previous chapter, Llŷr's name also translates to mean 'sea', meaning we could also translate Manawydan fab Llŷr to mean Manawydan, son of the Sea. Many Celticists such as Rachel Bromwich, John Rhŷs, and John MacCulloch have expressed the notion that Manawydan and Manannán are cognate with one another throughout their work. And so, perhaps we can learn something of Manawydan by looking to

Manannán, considering there seems to be a greater body of lore concerning Manannán than that of Manawydan.

The simplest way to understand Manawydan's name, and the approach most scholars today take, is to simply see it as the Welsh equivalent of Manannán. However, it could also possibly have links with the Welsh word *mynawyd*, which translates to mean an awl. An awl is a tool used to pierce holes through leather, often used by shoemakers. The notion that Manawydan's name may relate to such a tool is interesting, when one considers that shoemaking was one of the three crafts taken up by Manawydan during his time in England, the other two being shield making and saddle making. All three of these items: Shoes, saddles, and shields, are items that often incorporate leather into their design. Therefore, perhaps the notion that Manawydan's name has a link to a leather working tool makes a great deal of sense. Patrick Sims-Williams discusses this in his *Irish Influence on Medieval Welsh Literature* and proposes that perhaps *Mannan* or *Manaw* became contaminated with the Welsh *Mynawyd* in some later date, creating the word *Manawydan* and helping to establish the notion that the character Manawydan was a great craftsperson who worked with leather (Sims-Williams, 2011). Keep this idea of Manawydan being associated with an awl in mind, as we will return to it in a moment.

Manawydan becomes Rhiannon's second consort in the *Mabinogi*, after Pwyll's death. There are several hints of mysterious, magical goings on revolving around Rhiannon in the small portion of the text of the third branch which explains this binding. Firstly, a great many decades have transpired since the events of the second branch, and by the fact that Pryderi as a fully grown warrior was present in the second branch, we can ascertain it has been a long while since the events of the first branch too. We are led to believe that Pwyll simply died peacefully of old age, after a long and prosperous life. Manawydan and Pryderi, as two of the seven survivors of the events of the second branch spent seven years at Harlech feasting under the song of the Birds of Rhiannon. Then, after this, they spent another eighty years on Ynys Gwales entertained by Brân's head.

All this implies that Rhiannon is possibly over a century older than she was during the events of the first branch. Granted, if we consider the *Mabinogi* having a linear timeline. And yet, she is still very much described as being a beautiful, fair, and intelligent woman. Pryderi does note she is no longer in the prime of her life, and yet nothing said by him should cause us to believe she is an old crone, having lived over a hundred years. The events of the third branch imply she is very much energetic, agile, and regarded as incredibly beautiful. Perhaps a further hint to her divine or Otherworldly nature, that she is not affected much at all by the passing of time in the same way an ordinary mortal would.

Beyond this, in joining with Rhiannon in marriage Manawydan is given the right to rule over the seven cantrefs of Dyfed. Further evidence of Rhiannon's sovereignty. Surely by now, after Pwyll's death, Pryderi should have inherited the right to rule. And yet, in this simple act, the implication is that the right to rule can only be given to those who join in union with Rhiannon. When Pryderi tells Rhiannon of his plan to unite them in marriage, Rhiannon agrees gladly, impressed by Manawydan in many ways. She has chosen him as her consort, and now he takes the same role Pwyll had in the first branch.

It is interesting to compare Pwyll and Manawydan to one another. Pwyll is described in the first branch as often being hasty, diving into things too quickly, and his nature as someone who lacks caution and wisdom often lands him in trouble. Though, the trouble also teaches him a lesson and over the course of the first branch he eventually grows to be a competent, wise, successful leader. Manawydan on the other hand, from the very beginning, seems to embody caution, patience, wisdom, and is incredibly perceptive. He is perceptive to the presence and influence of Otherworldly forces. In the second branch, it is he who points out which door should not be opened on the Island of Gwales. When he and Pryderi follow a white boar into a thicket and discover a strange, unearthly towering fort, Manawydan warns that they should not enter the fort. It is Pryderi who rushes in against Manawydan's advice, almost mirroring his father's lack of caution and wisdom in such a situation.

Rhiannon initially criticises his cautious nature, seeing his refusal to follow Pryderi into the fort as a sign that he is not a true, loyal friend. And yet, when she takes matters into her own hands and does what she believes Manawydan should have done, she is trapped alongside Pryderi. Proving that Manawydan was correct to be cautious.

Pryderi's name can be translated to mean anxiety, and as someone who struggled with anxiety, I can attest that one thing anxiety leads me to do is jump to conclusions. To spin a narrative which is not based in any wisdom, caution, or forethought. These narratives that anxiety spin can often lead me to act in unwise ways. My anxiety will tell me that my friends don't truly like being in my company, and when I misguidedly trust that anxiety, I distance myself from them, which only causes more issues. Whereas the cautious side of my mind might tell me to instead be upfront and honest about my anxieties and insecurities, and often when I do just this I am reassured, and all is well. It is almost as though Pryderi embodies his name, throwing himself into situations which often lead him to trouble. When living in England and making a living via their craft local craftspeople threaten to kill Manawydan and Pryderi for taking away their business, Pryderi's solution to the problem is to kill them all himself. Manawydan instead states they should simply move to a new location and start again, and in following this advice they avoid any serious trouble. When Pryderi listens to Manawydan, things turn out well. When we temper our anxieties with caution and wise thought, we often stop ourselves from rushing into situations that will cause us more harm.

Manawydan is a prudent, cautious, perceptive, and wise man. He embodies these qualities well, even when many criticise him for doing so. Interestingly, if we harken back to the first branch and remind ourselves of the meaning behind Pwyll's name, we see that Manawydan can be described using this word. Manawydan embodies wisdom, and caution. In Welsh we would say that Manawydan embodies *Pwyll*.

Returning to the idea that Manawydan's name may have some reference to an awl, a device used to pierce through leather, I can easily see how we can draw on that idea to deepen our perception of him. An awl literally pierces a hole through tough, strong leather. It pierces through the physical, and once it has done so we can look through what was initially a material which would have blocked our view. By piercing the leather in this way, it then allows us to transform that raw material into something new. This is how I personally perceive Manawydan's role in the third branch, he offers a new perspective, one rooted in careful consideration. He pierces through the illusions that anxieties and our own insecurities can cast upon us, like an awl piercing through tough leather. Once this is done, we can approach our situations and our challenges from a new angle. We can transform it into something new, change the raw material into something far more useful and beneficial.

## The Waste Land...?

During the events of the third branch a great, horrid noise echoes across the landscape and a mist surrounds the characters. A dense white mist, which shrouds their vision. When the mist retreats, all signs of human life has vanished from Dyfed. No people, no buildings, no fences, no farm animals...all signs of humans, and of human civilisation have mysteriously vanished.

Leaving only our four primary characters: Manawydan, Pryderi, Rhiannon, and Cigfa.

When delving into the themes of the third branch of the *Mabinogi*, many writers will state that the primary story at hand, that of the enchantment of Dyfed, falls into a literary or folkloric motif known as a "waste land" story. Gruffydd, in his study of the first and second branches, titled *Rhiannon* argued that it is possible this branch was inspired by an older myth of a great Mother Goddess, who in the version of the tale we know today is echoed in Rhiannon, whose son is abducted, and as a result all life grinds to a halt (Gruffydd, 1953). It is important to note before I continue that Gruffydd's theories regarding the four branches are not widely accepted by academics today, still, Gruffydd is highly influential on the way in which scholars approach the *Mabinogi* today. This potential underlying mythology explained the need for the enchantment storyline in the third branch, according to Gruffydd.

The idea of the "waste land" motif harkens to classical mythology, such as that of Persephone's abduction, and how Demeter responded to the abduction by halting all growing life. The underlying theme of the waste land motif is the idea of the landscape growing infertile due to a particular event. This event is usually due to the failure of a monarch, or perhaps even because the monarch has been severely injured. Or, alternatively, as in Gruffydd's theory, it is due to the absence or grief of a fertility Goddess. The idea of the injured monarch causing the land to become infertile can be found in Arthurian legend, in the story surrounding the Fisher King, another tale often labelled under the waste land motif.

However, it must be noted that Dyfed during its enchantment is not a waste land at all. As pointed out by Andrew Welsh in his essay *Manawydan fab Llŷr: Wales, England, and the "new man"* (Welsh, 2020), the enchantment only truly takes away any semblance of human society. Yes buildings, cattle, human life, and man-made objects vanish, but the landscape is far from being infertile and barren. The tale itself makes it clear that the landscape is still abuzz with wild animals, honeybees, and fish. Manawydan and the gang depend on the land to survive in such a deserted landscape for at least two years before they set off to England. Their desire to leave seems rooted more in a desire for human company, and the comforts of human life than a need to leave in order to find food.

When Manawydan and Cigfa return from England after the second journey out of Dyfed, and after Rhiannon and Pryderi have been abducted, he brings seeds back to Dyfed. He sows the seeds, and the crops take to the soil beautifully, growing wheat in abundance. This does not seem to coincide with the notion that Dyfed is a barren, infertile waste land.

In the aforementioned essay by Andrew Welsh, he goes on to argue that it is in fact Manawydan's re-introduction of agriculture to Dyfed which sets the wheels in motion for the enchantment of the landscape to be lifted. I agree with this analysis.

I believe it is important to look at the third branch for what it truly is. The text makes it clear that we, as the reader, are supposed to think of this tale as following in a linear pattern after the events of the second branch. The second branch is one of intense destruction, upheaval, and unrest. In the aftermath of such events, the third branch is essentially a tale of re-building civilisation. Manawydan acts as the central figure to that re-building, and it is relevant to remember that he was present during the fighting in Ireland. He knows the evil and destruction that vengeance, and the desire to fight violent wars can bring.

Perhaps this speaks somewhat to Manawydan's nature. The third branch ends with Manawydan lifting the enchantment of Dyfed and demanding that the enchanter responsible for this and the abduction of Rhiannon and Pryderi vows not to seek vengeance after his defeat. He is the embodiment of a wise and successful king, and yet, not once did he lift a sword or turn to aggression or violence. Even with Pryderi and Cigfa goading him to kill the craftspeople in England who wished death upon them, he would not rise to aggression. Instead, he simply moves along, seeking the peaceful, cautious approach to challenges.

Manawydan drills the lesson of the second branch once more, that vengeance often leads only to destruction. Yes, perhaps the destruction of those who have wronged you, but at what cost? Who else, or what else, might be lost along the way? Fair words and carefully thought-out actions are often far superior to the striking of a sword, when it comes to solving a challenge.

## Magic and Enchantment in the Third Branch

When comparing the third branch to the other branches of the *Mabinogi*, it can often feel like the one with the least magic. I have met many people who dub this branch as their "least favourite", and when I enquire as to why, they will often tell me it is because of the lack of magical mischief at play. I can understand that to a degree, it certainly doesn't have as much of the otherworldly fanfare and cunning of the first branch, the dramatic war of the second branch with its giant King, cauldrons that re-animate the dead, and mystical islands where time does not affect on those dwelling there. And of course, compared to the fourth branch, a branch packed to the brim with magicians, transformations, and conjurations, it is easy to feel underwhelmed.

However, the third branch does indeed include magical themes, both overt and subtle in their nature. Let us explore some of these themes here, in hopes that anyone who feels disenchanted by the third branch may find themselves surprisingly enchanted once more.

The most overt example of magic in this branch, is that of the enchanted mist which descends upon Dyfed and leaves the landscape deserted. This mist, as we discover near to the close of the tale, is the work of a magician named Llwyd ap

Cil Coed. Whilst we could interpret Llwyd as being merely a mortal magician, akin to the magicians we will meet in the fourth branch, certain motifs and themes surrounding him and his magical acts hint towards him being Otherworldly in nature.

Firstly, there is the fact he admits to performing his magical acts as an act of vengeance in response to the disrespect shown to Gwawl ap Clud, who was formerly betrothed to Rhiannon, in the first branch. As a reminder, Gwawl was tricked by Pwyll to climb into Rhiannon's magical, seemingly bottomless bag. Once inside, Pwyll and his men played "badger in the bag" by beating and kicking him. By this admission alone, we can ascertain that Llwyd comes from the same place as Gwawl and Rhiannon, and based on certain motifs surrounding Rhiannon, such as her magical abilities, the fact we first see her dressed in golden brocaded silks, and her ageless nature, we can guess that they are from a Kingdom in Annwfn.

Keeping that in mind, and then remembering that he also has a seemingly magical fort which can appear out of nowhere, can conjure a magical mist, can change his shape, and is associated with a gleaming white boar, similar to the gleaming white dogs owned by Arawn, it draws a picture of an Otherworldly entity akin to Arawn.

Angelika Rüdiger in her thesis on fairies, published in 2021, draws parallels between the motifs surrounding Llwyd ap Cil Coed and folkloric beliefs associated with fairies. For example, folklorists such as Marie Trevelyan, E. Sydney Hartland, and Elias Owen discuss in their work a belief in a figure known as the 'Brenin Llwyd'. Brenin Llwyd can be translated to mean "the grey king", however, folklorists like to translate him into the "monarch of the mist". He is a King of the mountain mists, associated with fairy traditions, the Cŵn Annwn (Otherworldly hounds), and the abduction of people who stayed out too late in the mountains. His mists would descend upon those wandering the mountains late and cause them to become lost. It is easy to draw parallels between this fairy entity associated with dangerous mists, to Llwyd ap Cil Coed, an enchanter whose mists cause the disappearance of all semblances of human life and civilisation in Dyfed.

Despite him never saying so, it does appear, at least to me, that Manawydan is somehow aware that the enchantment of Dyfed is caused by Otherworldly forces. As we have already discussed, Manawydan is perceptive to the trickeries and illusions of the Otherworld. Beyond the examples we have already touched upon earlier in this chapter, there is also a mention in Welsh legendary verse that alludes to his association with the Otherworld. In the Taliesin poem *Golychaf-I Gulwyd* (I petition to God) an allusion is made to Manawydan.

> *Ys kyweir vyg kadeir yg Kaer Sidi:*
> *Nys plawd heint a heneint a uo yndi,*
> *Ys gwyr Manawyt a Phryderi*
> (Haycock, 2007)
> My song, it is harmonious in Caer Siddi,
> Those who are there are unafflicted by sickness and old age,
> As Manawydan and Pryderi know.
> (My own translation)

*Caer Sidi/Siddi* referenced in this poem refers to one of the forts of the Otherworld. We see Caer Siddi mentioned also in the poem *Preiddeu Annwn* (The Spoils of Annwfn) which describes an Otherworldly raid led by King Arthur. In the poem above, it seems to be implying either that Manawydan and Pryderi simply know that sickness and old age do not affect those in the Otherworld, or that Manawydan and Pryderi know the Otherworld intimately.

The former would make sense after the events of the second branch, but the latter would also make sense when one considers

The Third Branch

how perceptive Manawydan seems to be of the Otherworld, and the fact that Pryderi likely inherits his deceased father's title *Pen Annwfn* (Lord of the Otherworld). Both have ties to the Otherworld, and Pryderi's connection to Annwfn is only reiterated in the fourth branch when we learn that his territory still receives gifts from the King of the Otherworld.

Manawydan is unlike any of the magicians we see in the four branches. He does not wave a wand, any more than he waves a sword. And yet, there is a certain magical quality which emanates from him. When he catches the mouse, and goes forth to hang it, he acts almost as though he knows what he is doing. Though the text never says so, the entire episode of Manawydan catching, and attempting to punish the mouse as a thief, reads almost like a carefully crafted, cunning plan. As though he knew that endangering the mouse, who we later learn is Llwyd's pregnant wife transformed, would lure the antagonist of the story out.

This is even more evident, in my opinion, when Llwyd approaches Manawydan in disguise. No exchange occurs which points to the idea that the bishop Manawydan is speaking to has any sway on the fate of Dyfed, Rhiannon, or Pryderi. And yet, when the bishop asks him what he would like in return for the mouse's release, Manawydan is quick to ask for the release of Rhiannon and Pryderi, the disenchantment of Dyfed, and for Llwyd to vow that he will not take revenge for his defeat.

It is important I note here that this is all my own theory, but it seems Manawydan is a more cunning and competent magician than meets the eye. Though his perceptive, wise, cautious nature he singlehandedly lures Llwyd out of hiding, and bargains with him for all that he desires, and he achieves his goal. Dyfed is back to its former splendour, and the branch ends happily, all thanks to Manawydan. A successful King who shows that the sword is not the only weapon that can solve a problem. Wise words, careful consideration, and a dash of cunning can be just as, if not more effective.

# The Fourth Branch

Whilst the second branch is likely the most popular and well-known of the four branches in Welsh schools today, the fourth branch is undoubtably the most popular branch among modern day Pagans. This is the most overtly magical branch, with narratives focusing on animal transformations, wizards, and a woman conjured from flowers.

Once again, we see the theme of insult and reparation in this branch. Gwydion is often the cause behind most of the insults, whether he is insulting Pryderi, Math, or his own sister, Aranrhod. By the end of the branch, however, Gwydion is insulted himself, and lashes out at who he considers responsible.

It is easy to see why this branch would be so popular among Pagans and magical practitioners today. Whilst magic has been present for all three of the previous branches, it has mostly been a subtle force which alters the fate and fortune of the characters we follow. Yet here, in the fourth branch, magic is everywhere, and is often the solution to many problems. We have two contrasting magical characters — the rash, reckless, and flawed Gwydion, and the noble, just, and cautious Math. There is no undertone of a warning against magic here, for even Math, the great ruler of Gwynedd, is a skilled, proficient, and powerful magician. In this branch magic seems to be at the very beating heart of the culture of this landscape.

Let us now turn to the various themes and narratives at play in the fourth branch, and consider what wisdom we can glean from it.

## The War of the Pigs
Upon realising that Gilfaethwy is madly lustful for Goewin, the virgin which Math must always have his feet in the lap of, except when his kingdom is in conflict, Gwydion, in his impulsive

nature, concocts a plan to send the Kingdom of Gwynedd into conflict. A conflict with the territory ruled over by Pryderi.

Once again, we meet Pryderi, the son of Rhiannon and Pwyll, who, as the text explains, now rules over several territories in the South of Wales. There is no mention of Manawydan or Rhiannon, implying that Pryderi has since inherited the Lordship of Dyfed and also that his authority has expanded to other territories.

Another callback to the first branch comes in the mention that Pryderi and his people have received a wonderful gift from the King of Annwfn, Arawn. The gift is a drove of remarkable creatures, creatures which the Island of the Mighty has never seen before, creatures which taste better than beef. Pigs.

The fourth branch implies that swine are Otherworldly creatures, an interesting fact considering the appearance of a gleaming white boar in the previous branch, which led Pryderi into Llwyd's trap. Pigs would continue to be considered in many ways magical and otherworldly in later Welsh folklore. Elias Owen, a 19th century Welsh antiquarian and folklorist notes in his *Welsh Folk-Lore* how pigs were believed in many parts of Wales to have uncanny abilities. These uncanny abilities included being able to see the wind, and that Devils and Otherworldly spirits often took the form of pigs (Owen, 1887).

Gwydion uses the fact that Pryderi's territories have these special creatures, and Gwynedd does not, to manipulate Math into allowing him to travel to Pryderi's court with the intention of securing some pigs for his uncle's kingdom. However, his true motive is to stir up conflict, in hopes that Math will be able to take his feet away from Goewin's lap, and his brother Gilfaethwy would have the chance to sleep with her.

After travelling down to Pryderi's court at Rhuddlan Teifi, Gwydion manages to trick Pryderi, via enchantment and manipulation, into giving him pigs. This sets events into motion, for when Pryderi realises he has been tricked, conflict erupts between the men of the South and the men of the North.

Initially it seems as though an all-out war similar to that of the second branch may begin. However, Pryderi seems reluctant to allow too many to fight and die to solve his issue. Here we potentially see a connection between the first and second branches yet again. Pryderi requests that this conflict be resolved with a battle between himself and Gwydion. This is reminiscent of the battle between Arawn and Hafgan in the first branch, a battle Pryderi's father aided in winning for Arawn. Perhaps Pryderi also preferred the idea that Gwydion and himself fight out their differences in order to avoid the devastation on the level of the second branch. After all, he was one of the seven survivors, and likely carries the trauma of the memory of such events.

Pryderi, however, was likely foolish to challenge Gwydion. For Gwydion is more than merely a proficient and skilled warrior, he is also a practitioner of magic. Skilled in the arts of enchantment, Gwydion wins the battle not just because of his strength but also thanks to his magic. Finally, here, at the start of the fourth branch, the one character who had a role in all four branches meets his end.

Pryderi is buried at a place called Maentwrog, above Y Felenrhyd. One thing I have always personally adored about the four branches of the *Mabinogi*, is the fact that they are so deeply rooted in locality. The events of the tales do not happen in a land far, far away, a long, long time ago. Growing up we were always led to believe that the landscape around us, our childhood playgrounds, were the very locations of these events. Having grown up in the North we often visited places with association to the *Mabinogi*, and so these stories and their interesting characters always felt near and familiar, like extended family, ancestors of the sacred landscape.

Woven into the fact that the places mentioned in the *Mabinogi* would be familiar to Welsh folks, is the onomastic elements to

The stories. Throughout the branches we have received several explanations as to why places are called what they are called. In the second branch it is explained how Talybolion, an area which is now on Ynys Cybi off the coast of Anglesey, was named this because it is where Matholwch received his compensation of horses after Efnysien's horrid insult. Talybolion translates to essentially mean "payment of the horses". And here in the fourth branch we see yet another onomastic reference, this time to a great many places across the width and breadth of Wales.

Across Wales there are places which carry the word *moch* in their names. *Moch* means swine, or pigs. Several place names are called *Mochdref* meaning the town of the pigs, and we also have *Mochnant* meaning the valley or the dale of the pigs. According to this branch, these places got their names after Gwydion and the men of Gwynedd stopped at these places on their way home from tricking Pryderi into giving them the pigs.

As Sioned Davies explains in her *Pedeir Keinc y Mabinogi*, whilst it is easy to view Gwydion as a manipulative and wicked trickster responsible for all the strife in this branch, ultimately Pryderi's death was of his own doing (Davies, 1989). Pryderi had pledged a covenant with his people regarding the pigs, a promise was made and whilst yes, Gwydion tricked him by promising him ever so much, that covenant or promise was broken out of a desire for more. The second branch taught us that seeking vengeance often only leads to chaos, and even death. Here, we are taught another moral lesson, how important it is to keep a promise or to hold true to one's words. For to venture away from your own obligation to keep such vows is a surefire method of ensuring one's own destruction.

However, Pryderi was simply a pawn of the greater game Gwydion was playing in inciting this conflict. His primary reason for sending Gwynedd into battle with the men of the South, was to pry Math's feet away from the lap of his foot maiden, which Gwydion's brother madly wanted. They succeeded in doing this, and eventually Goewin was taken by force. A hideous and wicked act, and one which would leave Gwydion and Gilfaethwy facing a peculiar sort of punishment.

## Math and Gwydion – The Cautious and the Reckless

Upon hearing what vile things Gwydion and Gilfaethwy have been up to, the Lord of Gwynedd, Math, who also happens to be a powerful magician decides to punish the brothers in an interesting manner. Over a long period of time the brothers are transformed into mating animals. A stag and a hind, a boar and a sow, a wolf and a she-wolf. They take on the very nature of these creatures, and mate in order to create a fawn, a boarlet, and a cub. These children are transformed into human form and named Bleiddwn, Hyddwn, and Hychddwn hir.

The names given to Gwydion and Gilfaethwy's children are rather interesting. The first is Hyddwn, conceived by Gwydion and Gilfaethwy in the form of a stag and a hind. The name Hyddwn includes the word *Hydd* meaning stag or hart. This style follows for all three children, with Hychddwn including the word *Hych* from *Hwch* meaning a sow or pig, and Bleiddwn including the word *Bleidd* from *Blaidd* meaning wolf. Their names carry an element of the forms from which they were originally created, and perhaps this implies that their nature correlates in some way with the nature of these animals as well.

Once again in this branch we see the theme of insult and reparation rear its head. This time the insult has been thrown towards Math, and it is a fairly large insult at that. Math has a taboo upon his life, this taboo dictates that he must always have his feet in the lap of a virgin in order to live. The only time he can remove his feet from the lap of a virgin is during times of conflict, when his territory is at war. Gwydion concocted the entire conflict in the first part of this branch purely to pull Math away from his foot maiden, Goewin, so that his brother Gilfaethwy could have the chance to sleep with her. In doing so Gwydion has not only endangered the entire kingdom of Gwynedd, and violated a woman against her will, but he has also threatened Math's life in the process. With that in mind, the punishment given to Gwydion and Gilfaethwy seems light.

In this first escapade alone, we see the juxtaposition between Math and Gwydion, two important characters who happen to be magicians. Math follows in the tradition of Manawydan in being a ruler who cares for his land with a cautious, wise, and gentle nature. His primary method of ruling relies on a compassion and care for his people, his family, and his landscape, rather than by brute strength or by his skill with a sword. When Gwydion brings conflict to the land, Math's first instinct is to protect his people, stating he does not wish to send any of his people into battle if it is not absolutely necessary.

Upon discovering what Gwydion and Gilfaethwy have done to his foot maiden, Math's initial concern is the well-being and future of Goewin. Before he worries about punishing the brothers, before he is concerned with his own life and his need to find a new virgin to place his feet in the lap of, he tends to the one who has been wronged the most.

In these qualities we once again see a leader elevated to exemplify the role of the "ideal King". Just as Brân in the second branch, and Manawydan in the third represented an ideal leader, Math does so here. He is just, fair, and a skilled magician and King.

As you have likely realised by now, we can learn a lot about the characters of the four branches by delving into the etymology and meaning behind their names. However, when it comes to Math this is a little difficult. Whilst the word *math* is a word in modern Welsh, meaning 'sort' or 'variety', it is unlikely that this is the meaning behind Math's name, as the usage of the word *math* in this manner does not appear in Welsh written record until at least the 16th century. What is more likely is that Math is a very old name, especially considering it shares a resemblance to names we see in both Irish and Gaulish culture (Bromwich, 2014). In Irish lore the Druid of the Tuatha Dé Dannan in the Lebor Gabála is named Math Mac Umóir. Being a Druid, this character shares a commonality with Math as being a highly respected leader of sorts, associated with magic or spiritual prowess.

One thing that is certain about Math is his status as a great magician. He can work great magic with his magic wand, and he hears all things caught by the wind. Beyond this tale in the four branches, Math's magical prowess is emphasised in the triads and in legendary poems. He is mentioned in Triad number 28, which glorifies Math as being one of the three most notable and powerful magicians of Britain alongside Uther Pendragon and Rudlwm the dwarf (Bromwich, 2014). This triad also mentions how he passed his magic on to Gwydion, implying that Gwydion was trained in the art of enchantment by his uncle.

Where Math is powerful yet cautious and considerate, Gwydion is powerful and reckless. Throughout this branch he proves time and time again that he rushes into situations without much forethought. He acts as almost the polar opposite of Math, and his solutions to the issues that arise before him often lead to nothing but disaster and chaos. When his brother is infatuated with a woman who seems unobtainable, his solution is to imperil Gwynedd and his Uncle Math, and then violate her against her will. Kristoffer Hughes, in his *The Book of Celtic Magic* refers to Gwydion as 'The Flawed Magician' (Hughes, 2014) and discusses how Gwydion and his escapades can act as a lesson to those of us who practice magic today, reminding us to act with caution, consideration, wisdom, and care before turning to magic. It is easy to run to what might appear to be the easiest solution to problems, however, the easiest solution is not necessarily always the wisest or most beneficial.

There is evidence towards the idea that Gwydion once had a greater depth of lore in Welsh culture than what we now have preserved. Several poems attributed to the legendary Taliesin refer to him. Likely the most infamous of his appearances is in the poem known as the *Kat Godeu*, or the Battle of the Trees. In this poem, via his mastery of language and of magic, Gwydion raises an army of trees to fight in an epic battle. With wand in hand, he commands the great host of Alder, Willow, Rowan, and Blackthorn trees to name but a few. Each tree has its own identity and virtue in this battle.

Gwydion may be reckless, flawed, and we could even perceive him as lacking in principles, but it is clear that he is a highly skilled and powerful magician. Here in the fourth branch, he fools Pryderi with his illusions, transforming toadstools into shields, and conjuring dogs and horses out of thin air. And yet, beyond his magic, his tongue is also one of his greatest weapons. A great storyteller, and an expert manipulator. It is his mastery of language and of magic which define who Gwydion is, and the power he holds in his lore.

There are many ways in which we can explore his name and its possible meaning. For example, his name may share an etymological root with the word *Gwybod* which means 'to know'. If this is correct, then we can perceive him as being the knowledgeable one, he who knows many things. Following on that logic, his name may also be linked with the word *gwŷdd* which can be translated to mean knowledge or science. However, the word *Gwŷdd* also translates to mean trees, woods, or a forest. The fact he is associated with trees in Welsh lore might indicate that his name might refer to his role as a caller or conjurer of the army of trees.

Gwydion and Math exist as two sides of the same coin. A lesson in good leadership, and responsible weaving of magic, versus a chaotic, reckless, and foolish way of being. Math is seen as a good and kind leader, successful in his authority, whereas Gwydion is repeatedly attempting to clean up messes he has caused himself. Gwydion seems to have little control over his own magic nor his own actions. Later in the branch, events become once again chaotic when he turns to magic to help Lleu in finding a wife. Time and time again we are reminded that Gwydion acts without much caution, and this leads him and those around him into peril and trouble.

## Aranrhod – That Which Sets the Wheel in Motion

After Gwydion and Gilfaethwy have violated Math's foot holder, he is in need of a new virgin to rest his feet upon the lap of. Gwydion, in what is likely an attempt to rectify his wrongdoing, offers up his sister, Aranrhod. Unfortunately, chaos ensues once again when, upon stepping over Math's magic wand, Aranrhod gives birth to a golden-haired child, proving that she is not a virgin. She runs out of Math's court, deeply embarrassed and ashamed, and as she does, she births another thing. Gwydion grabs this thing and keeps it in a chest at the end of his bed. Before long, the thing becomes another child.

This is our introduction to Aranrhod, a character who would become one of the most popular among modern Pagans from all of Welsh mythology. Aranrhod, or as she is more commonly known outside of Wales, Arianrhod, has become a well-known name among Pagans and Witches today. Several Neopagan books mention her as a Goddess, one that Witches in particular are incredibly fond of. And yet, the Arianrhod of Neopaganism seems to have a persona rather divorced from the character found here in the *Mabinogi*.

Gerald Gardner himself, father of Wicca, referred to Arianrhod in his book *The Meaning of Witchcraft*. In it he describes Arianrhod as the daughter of Dôn, but then goes on to say that she was a moon goddess, and that the souls of fallen heroes journeyed to her castle after death (Gardner, 1959). Since him, many authors who write on the subject of modern Paganism and Witchcraft have written about Arianrhod in a similar manner. Janet and Stewart Farrar referred to Arianrhod as a Goddess who rules over a castle which is located beyond the North Wind, where all souls who are journeying between life and death must visit (Farrar & Farrar, 1987). In Marguerite Elsbeth and Kenneth Johnson's *The Silver Wheel*, a book which explores women's myths and mysteries in the Celtic tradition, Arianrhod's Castle rears its head again as the place which rests between life and death, and Arianrhod sits as a Goddess of the skies and the waves, a woman suppressed under the boot of patriarchy, which takes manifest form as her brother and her uncle, Math and Gwydion (Elsbeth & Johnson, 1997).

It seems clear by looking at these sources that Arianrhod has long been perceived by modern day Pagans and Witches as a Goddess of the moon, and a guardian of sorts whose court acts as a liminal space between the living world and the afterlife. This is the perception of Arianrhod I often come across from Pagans and Witches I meet, especially those who perhaps were not raised with the four branches of the *Mabinogi*. But is this truly who Arianrhod is in Welsh lore?

The castle referenced in all three examples above is Caer Arianrhod (Arianrhod's Fort). In the fourth branch, this is where Arianrhod is said to reside, in a court named after her. It is interesting to note at this point that Arianrhod seems to have an air of independence and agency that is sorely missing in many of the other women of the four branches. Rhiannon, as fierce and cunning as she is, is seemingly identified in the texts by her relation to both her father, Hyfaidd Hen, and to her consorts, Pwyll in the first branch, and Manawydan in the third. Whilst she certainly has an identity of her own and is not entirely defined by her relation to these men, they are still very much a crucial part of her identity in the tales. The same can be said of Branwen, who is referred to as Branwen ferch Llŷr (the daughter of Llŷr) and is given in marriage to Matholwch by her brother, Brân. But Arianrhod is never truly identified in relation to a man. Beyond being the sister of Gwydion, and the niece of Math, she is never referred to as being the daughter of a specific man, nor is her court named after a man. Her court is named after her, indicating it is her land, and that she has an air of authority which is entirely her own.

In this branch, nothing much is said of her fort, Caer Arianrhod, beyond that it is where she dwells and that it is likely located on an island out at sea. If we were to look beyond the four branches, to legendary poems, we see reference to it in a poem titled *Kadeir Kerrituen* (The Chair of Cerridwen). In this poem Caer Arianrhod is described as a court surrounded by a raging river (Haycock, 2007).

Caer Arianrhod certainly has a hold on Welsh culture, for there are two distinct places in the real world which bear this name to this day. The first is a large reef located off the coast of Gwynedd. At extremely low tide, this reef is visible, and looks like rough rocks jutting out of the sea but is otherwise submerged beneath the waves most of the time. From where I grew up, on the Isle of Anglesey, this reef is sometimes visible from Ynys Llanddwyn, a short distance from the village I was raised in, and so I grew up with stories of the court of Arianrhod, which at some point in time fell beneath the waves of the sea.

The second place referred to as Caer Arianrhod is not located on land nor sea, but in the sky. The Corona Borealis carries the name Caer Arianrhod in Wales, and this is interesting as she is not the only one of her family to have her name and court preserved in the stars. Caer Gwydion, the Fort of Gwydion, is the milky way, and Cassiopeia is Llys Dôn. It seems Dôn and her children share courts among the stars.

However, despite all this, there is still no mention in Welsh lore of Arianrhod's fort being a liminal space between life and death, where souls, whether they be fallen heroes or otherwise, venture to between this life and the next.

It seems that this idea originates not in Welsh lore, but in the work of English poet and novelist Robert Graves. In his work *The White Goddess* Graves discusses the idea of the 'spiral castle', a place where kings and heroes arrive after death. After ruminating on the idea that Arianrhod and Cerridwen are the same entity, and referring to Arianrhod as a Goddess of life and death, Graves goes on to say this:

*"To be in the Castle of Arianrhod is to be in a royal purgatory awaiting resurrection"* (Graves, 1948)

And so, the puzzle is solved. Whilst there is nothing in Welsh lore to directly state that Arianrhod is a Goddess who awaits souls on the transition between life, death, and reincarnation, this is how Graves interpreted her based on his readings of the *Mabinogi*. It seems his ideas became muddled with the Welsh texts, and now it has become a standard belief among Pagans, repeated over and over again. However, whilst this explains where the idea of Caer Arianrhod being a purgatory where souls rest before reincarnation, it does not explain why she is also known by many Pagans today as a moon Goddess.

The only indication in Welsh lore that Arianrhod might be associated with the moon is due to her name. Arianrhod is comprised of the words *Arian* meaning silver, and *Rhod* meaning wheel. And so, it is clear to see how many might draw a link between "silver wheel" and the moon. However, is that truly what Arianrhod's name translates to mean?

At the start of this section, I referred to this character not as Arianrhod, but as Aranrhod, and that was no error. Aranrhod is the modern Welsh equivalent to a version of this name preserved in the medieval manuscripts, in middle Welsh the spelling was *Aranrot*. Occasionally the spelling of this name is instead *Aryanrot*, which would be Arianrhod in modern Welsh.

However, it is important to note that Aranrot/Aranrhod is the more consistent spelling (Bromwich, 2014).

It is important to note here that if her name is indeed Aranrhod, and not Arianrhod, then this changes the meaning of her name entirely. The rot/rhod stays consistent in both versions, and this word denotes a wheel. However, Aran does not translate to mean 'silver' as Arian does. There have been a few ideas as to the exact meaning of Aran. Rachel Bromwich in *Trioedd Ynys Prydein* notes that the word Aran is preserved in the names of mountain peaks, and that the meaning of it is likely along the lines of "huge", "round", or "humped" (Bromwich, 2014).

Welsh scholar Sir Ifor Williams, however, drew a link between the words *aran* and *garan* (Williams, 1930). The Welsh language has woven into our grammatical rules what we refer to as *treigladau*, the only English equivalent word to explain this grammatical rule is 'mutation'. Words mutate and change depending on the grammar of a sentence. In certain circumstances the word *garan* would mutate to *aran*. Now, the word *garan* refers to an axle, that is a rod or a spindle which passes through the centre of a wheel in order to allow it to move.

Considering Aranrhod's name has the wheel association in the suffix -*rhod* it seems logical that the prefix would have some significance to this theme. And so, if Sir Ifor Williams was correct in drawing a connection between *aran* and *garan* it would imply then that rather than 'silver wheel', Aranrhod's name instead translates to mean 'the axle of the wheel'. Or, if we are to take poetic license, 'that which allows the wheel to turn' or 'the still point at the centre of the wheel'. I prefer this interpretation of the meaning behind her name, and also the spelling 'Aranrhod' more so than 'Arianrhod'.

Whether the name is wheel's axle, or large/humped wheel, all of this just goes to prove that Aranrhod's name is complex. And it seems that the entire notion that she is a 'moon Goddess' lays solely on the fact that her name translates to mean 'silver wheel'. Nothing else in the lore pertaining to Aranrhod implies she has a connection to the moon.

We have spent a lot of time now discussing who Aranrhod is outside of Welsh culture, and the seemingly large departure from her original character. So, who is she actually? Within the fourth branch?

Aranrhod is an interesting character in that she seems to reject the expectations placed upon her as a woman. Roberta L. Valente wrote an essay in 1996 on the subject of the theme of crossing gender boundaries in the fourth branch of the *Mabinogi*. In said essay, Valente outlines how gender roles are expressed in a rather straightforward manner throughout all four branches. The role of the man is to govern the land, protect the people, and marry a woman in order to have children who might continue their legacy, whereas women are often defined by their role in relation to said men (Valente, 1996). It is likely that these gender roles express the usual roles of men and women in medieval Wales, and whilst many of the characters throughout all four branches, especially the women, can be interpreted as breaking out of the usual expectations placed upon women, no one does it as overtly as Aranrhod.

The moment Aranrhod is proven not to be a virgin, when she gives birth to a child after stepping over Math's wand, she abandons the child, rushing out of the room. It is instead Math who takes notice of the child, and names it, before it makes for the sea and takes on the nature of the water itself. When Gwydion comes to her with another child later, she resists his efforts to try and force her to conform to what is expected of her. She outright rejects her role as a mother, retreating to her fortress, essentially wishing and acting as though the child does not exist.

It is instead Gwydion who seems to take on the traditionally feminine role in this part of the branch. After the birth of Dylan, the golden-haired boy who makes for the waves not long after receiving a name from Math, another "thing" drops from within Aranrhod as she takes her leave. Gwydion takes this "thing" and places it in a chest at the foot of his bed. The chest acts as a kind of magical incubator, and before long it transforms into a child and is birthed into the world.

This entire scene almost hints at the idea that the child is the creation of both Aranrhod and Gwydion, but it is in Gwydion's chest that the child is grown to term, not in a woman's womb.

Throughout the rest of this branch Aranrhod makes her feelings towards this child, which she rejects as her own, incredibly clear. She refers to him as a *kywilyd* a word modern Welsh speakers would recognise as *cywilydd* which denotes shame, disgrace, or dishonour. That is all the child is to her, a burden, a reminder of the shame she endured. She cannot be shoved into a box as a caring, loving mother. In fact, she seems to point blank refute being perceived or labelled as a mother.

To emphasise her hatred of the idea of being a mother to this child even further, and her anger towards Gwydion who is attempting to force her to acknowledge the obligation he perceives she has, she places *tyngedau* on the child.

It is difficult to fully translate the word *tynged*, many have tried, but a translation never fully meets the essence of the term. Some translate it to mean curse, others fate. Essentially a *tynged* is a taboo placed upon your life, if you have a *tynged* placed upon you it is difficult for it to ever be broken. We could perhaps perceive the fact that Math needs to have his feet in the lap of a virgin as a *tynged*.

The *tyngedau* placed upon the child are ruthless and harsh. He shall never have a name, he shall never carry weapons, and he shall never marry a woman of mortal stock. All three things a man would have needed in order to thrive and survive. Without a name he is no one, without weapons he cannot protect himself, without a wife he cannot have children or a family. He would be nothing more than a spectre, roaming the landscape, in peril, and anonymity all his life. However, Gwydion manages to break these *tyngedau* via his manipulation, trickery, and magic. The child becomes Lleu Llaw Gyffes.

All this has led to Aranrhod being perceived as nothing more than a vile villain, a block in the path of the ascent of Lleu Llaw Gyffes, a hero who would one day become a great lord. Personally, however, I perceive her differently. To me, she is a woman who stands in her own power, authority, and autonomy. She rejects any ideas of what she 'should' be, and instead embraces all that she truly is. One issue I have with her role in modern Paganism as a moon Goddess, who dwells on a mystical island where souls go to rest prior to being reincarnated, is that it is so far removed from who she is in Welsh lore. This is a shame because I believe she is deeply interesting as she is. There is so much we could read into her story and her characterisation. She is a woman who chafes against the norm. I would think those who identify as Witches today might feel a kinship with such a woman. This is why I struggle with those who wish to force her into boxes such as "Moon Goddess", or heaven forbid "Mother Goddess", as it seems to directly go against who she is within Welsh lore.

## Lleu and Blodeuedd – Skilful Light, and Untameable Nature

The closing episode of the fourth branch is likely the most well-known, and the most popular today. After Gwydion presented Aranrhod's child to her, and she placed the three *tyngedau* upon him, Gwydion eventually tricked Aranrhod into breaking those *Tyngedau* herself. Her third and final *tynged,* however, would prove difficult. Aranrhod made it so that Lleu Llaw Gyffes could never have a wife that is of mortal stock. With this new predicament in place, Gwydion calls to the aid of Math, his mentor in magic, and concocts a plan to conjure a woman out of flowers. Let us now explore two more characters from this branch, Lleu Llaw Gyffes and Blodeuedd.

Lleu Llaw Gyffes received his name via trickery, Aranrhod named him herself, whilst he was under an enchantment and unrecognisable to her. She named him Lleu Llaw Gyffes after she witnessed him skilfully hit a wren. He is named for his precise skill, Llaw Gyffes, which translates to 'skilful hand'. However, the first part of his name, *Lleu* is one I have found often stumps people. The primary reason for the confusion as to Lleu's name is due to the fact that earlier translations of the *Mabinogi* into English have his name down as Llew Llaw Gyffes, rather than Lleu. Lleu and Llew may seem fairly similar but are two completely different words in Welsh.

Llew is how the name appears most commonly in the manuscripts, save for a few examples where it is written as Lleu. This should imply that Lleu is correct, if it were not for the fact that there is proof to say otherwise. Whilst Llew is the more consistent spelling, when his name appears in the *englynion*, the bardic verses sang by Gwydion, the words that are meant to rhyme with his name according to the poetic metre of the verses end with an *-eu* sound as opposed to an *-ew* sound. This leads many to believe that Lleu is the correct form, not Llew (Bromwich, 2014).

If his name was indeed Llew Llaw Gyffes, then the translation of his name would be something along the lines of "the Lion of Skilful Hand". However, if we are to perceive his name instead as Lleu, then it has nothing to do with a lion. We can find the sound *Lleu* or similar in various Welsh words today, for example — Gol*eu*ni, *Lleu*ad. These are words for light and the moon. Lleu essentially denotes brightness, light, or specifically rays of light. And so, rather than lion, his name would translate to mean light. Light of Skilful Hand, Lleu Llaw Gyffes.

In need of a wife, but unable to get one due to the *tynged* placed upon him by Aranrhod, Gwydion and Math conjure a woman out of flowers. Oak, Broom, and Meadowsweet combine to create a woman named Blodeuedd. Her name means "of the flowers", and she is the flowers of the forest brought to life, existing within human form.

Blodeuedd's entire purpose is to be Lleu's wife, her existence relies on her fulfilling that function and role. However, she has her own mind, her own identity, and she is unhappy and unfulfilled in this pre-determined role. Blodeuedd becomes the unfaithful wife of the story, cast as an adulterous villain who sleeps with another man, Gronw Pebr, and worse, together they plot to kill Lleu.

It is easy to frame this story as one of a wicked adulterous wife, a story akin to Adam and Eve, where Eve is coaxed away from her paradisical world and the role she was supposedly born to perform, towards temptation, a temptation which would reap consequences beyond her own life. However, over the past few decades this story has gained international love as being a feminist story. The story of a woman who refuses to bend to the will of the patriarchal world she is trapped within. A woman who wishes to have control over her own identity, autonomy, and fate. When she dares break free of the mould men have forced her into, she is punished, transformed into an owl. Once her shape is transformed, so to is her name. No longer is she Blodeuedd "of the flowers", she is now Blodeuwedd "flower face". The name Blodeuwedd refers to the fact that an owl's face looks like a flower.

One thing I find important to acknowledge is that Blodeuedd was more than simply a woman forced into a role placed upon her by men. She was a being of the wild, the flowers of the forest transformed into human form. Whilst I think a reading of her story as one of the plights of women is needed, how this world will often punish women for daring to attempt to carve out our own path, we could also perceive it as a metaphor for how, try as we might, we cannot conquer the natural world. Blodeuedd always reminds me of those images you see floating around online of ruins of man-made structures completely reclaimed by nature. Cracked concrete with plants sprouting out from the soil beneath it, abandoned churches overtaken by vines and creeping plants, trees bursting through the middle of what was once a building. Blodeuedd, in my eyes, also acts as a reminder that try as we might, it is near impossible to change something, or someone's innate nature. Their true expression will always break through, eventually. Just as one day our perfectly manicured concrete jungles, built to keep the natural world out, will crumble, and nature will reclaim them.

The fourth branch is filled with the most delicious of wisdom and lore. It is difficult to determine what parts of the tale to focus on. As with all the branches, take your time wading through the narratives at play here, and see what wisdom you might draw from them.

# Beyond the Four Branches

As mentioned in this book's introduction, if you purchase a copy of the *Mabinogi* today, usually under the title of *The Mabinogion*, you will find within its pages more than just the four branches. Depending on the version you purchase, there will be a total of eleven or more tales included in the collection.

This book focused on the four branches, the 'Mabinogi Proper' so to speak. However, I felt it necessary to at least touch upon these other prose tales often grouped alongside the four branches and provide a little insight as to what these tales are.

The tales found alongside the four branches are prose tales which have been preserved in the same manuscripts as the *Mabinogi* tales. Whilst they are part and package of the same literary Welsh tradition as the *Mabinogi*, they do not fit into an organic grouping with the four branches. The four branches are clearly a group of tales meant to be explored alongside one another. The scribes made certain to make that as clear as day by giving them a shared name, the *Mabinogi*, placing them into 'branches', and ending them all with the same statement 'and thus ends this branch of the Mabinogi'. The word 'Mabinogi' is never used in these other prose tales. They do not follow any form of seriality to the four branches it seems, and though there are brief references here and there to characters touched upon in the four branches, none of the primary characters of any individual story are those from the four branches.

Further, the world presented in these other prose tales tends to be far removed from the one presented in the four branches. In these tales we no longer have an image of ancient Wales, the Island of the Mighty. Instead, in some of these tales we are presented with a world which seems closer to continental romances, and others seem to deal with historical events expressing an insight into the formation of what would become Wales as the redactor knew it.

There have been many attempts to categorise these tales under a simple catch-all name similar to 'Mabinogi'. However, because they are all so vastly different to one another, and explore various themes, this is proven difficult. In modern academia the term Mabinogion, the scribal error under which these prose tales have been popularised, is used to describe the four branches and these other tales as a somewhat cohesive collection. Other attempts have attempted to section these tales into further categories, labelling some as 'Romances' and others as 'Native Tales'.

The tales referred to traditionally as the 'Romances' are so-called because they share rather deep similarities with the 12th century romances of Chrétien de Troyes. These tales are:

Peredur fab Efrawg – Peredur son of York
Geraint fab Erbin – Geraint son of Erbin
Iarlles y Ffynnon – The Lady of the Well

These tales are viewed as corresponding to Chrétien de Troyes' *Perceval*, *Erec et Enide*, and *Yvaine*. Sioned Davies notes how, whilst it is incredibly likely these tales are indeed loose retellings of the Chrétien de Troyes romances, they should not be considered as merely copies or reproductions. They have been adapted to fit into Welsh culture, and as such have themes and narrative structures which hold a native expression (Davies, 2007). Essentially, whilst they hold an echo of continental romantic flare, they are still at their heart an expression of the literary and storytelling culture of Wales.

The remaining tales are often described as 'Native Tales' in comparison to the Romances. This is misleading and indeed rather unsuitable. These groupings would imply that the three 'Romances' are nothing but pale imitations of another culture's stories, whereas the remaining tales are truly 'ours'. An idea which diminishes the inherently Welsh nature of the stories designated as 'Romances' under this attempt at categorisation.

The tales dubbed as 'Native Tales' sometimes include Arthurian tales, which seem to present a version of the legendary King Arthur far removed from the Arthur of the European continent and the Arthur of what would become later Arthurian tradition. They harken to a Britain ruled over by the mighty King Arthur who rules from his court in Cornwall. The other tales, which do not feature Arthur, deal with themes relating to British history. They explore a folkloric presentation of early British history, dealing with characters such as Lludd, a King of Britain before the Roman invasion, and Macsen, who is based on the historical Magnus Maximus, a fourth century Roman emperor who became rather important in perceptions of Welsh history.

The tales under the category of 'Native Tales' within this system are as follows:

Breuddwyd Macsen – The Dream of the Emperor Maxen
Lludd a Llefelys – Lludd and Llefelys
Culhwch ac Olwen – How Culhwch won Olwen
Breuddwyd Rhonabwy – Rhonabwy's Dream

These seven tales, alongside the four branches of the *Mabinogi*, comprise what we dub today as *'The Mabinogion'*. A term which has no historical grounding as one which defines these tales as a collection, but instead has become an easy catch-all to refer to these prose tales as a collection or group. These are the early prose tales of Wales, preserved for us to explore within the medieval manuscript tradition.

But wait, you might be saying, what about the tale concerning the legendary bard Taliesin? The story which includes Cerridwen, a powerful Witch who brewed a potion of Awen? Where does that tale fit, and why haven't I mentioned it as of yet?

Whether or not the tale of Taliesin is included depends on the translation you might have. Certain translations will include it, such as the Lady Charlotte Guest collection, and the translation offered by Patrick K. Ford. Whereas others will not include it, such as the Sioned Davies version, or the Welsh language Dafydd and Rhiannon Ifans version. So why is this? Why do some translators and scholars choose to include it where others do not?

The simple answer to this question is that the Taliesin text does not fit neatly into the same tradition as the four branches of the *Mabinogi* and the other prose tales.

The earliest and most complete version of the Taliesin tale comes to us from a 16th century manuscript, Elis Gruffudd's *Chronicles of the History of the World*. When compared to the four branches and other prose tales compiled into collections today known as '*The Mabinogion*', this 16th century tale is a far later text. The tale is relegated to the land of 'Folk-Tale' today. However, it is important to note, that whilst the story in its entirety cannot be found in earlier manuscripts, many references and echoes woven into earlier poetry and prose seems to imply that this story, in some form or other, is indeed far older than the 16th century (Hughes, 2021).

However, due to its peculiar nature as being perceived as nothing more than a later folk tale, preserved in a much later manuscript, many will choose to forego including it in their collection of translations today. Whether or not it should be categorised under the title of '*Mabinogion*' depends on who it is you ask.

Perhaps one day I shall write a book which explores these further prose tales, beyond the *Mabinogi*, in further detail.

# A Guide to Welsh Pronunciation

For those who have no experience of hearing the Welsh language being spoken, the names, place names, and certain words mentioned throughout this book may seem daunting. How does one pronounce *Pwyll* or *Manawydan*? Whilst the Welsh language may seem daunting, fear not! The rules of pronunciation are fairly simple, and once you know said rules, you will be able to learn to read Welsh words with ease.

Welsh is a phonetic language, and therefore once you learn how to pronounce each letter in the alphabet, it is fairly easy to deduce how a word should sound. In the English language one singular letter may be pronounced several different ways. For example, the word *Aggravating* in English has three a's, and the sound the a makes is different on all three occasions. The first is an 'ah' sound, the second an 'uh' sound, and the third an 'ay' sound. This is incredibly rare in the Welsh language. Once you have discovered the sound a letter makes, it is likely that letter will always sound that way. For example, A in the Welsh alphabet is pronounced 'Ah'. So, whether you see an A in words such as *Afal* (apple), *Aros* (wait), or *Annwfn* (The Otherworld) that 'A' in all these words is pronounced 'Ah'.

Keeping this in mind, one of the easiest methods of learning how to pronounce words in Welsh relatively quickly, is to familiarise yourself with the Welsh alphabet.

## The Welsh Alphabet
a, b, c, ch, d, dd, e, f, ff, g, ng, h, i, l, ll, m, n, o, p, ph, r, rh, s, t, th, u, w, y

As I have mentioned, it is very rarely that a word will change its pronunciation in Welsh, especially when compared to English. This makes learning pronunciations easier. However, I keep stating that it is 'rare' a letter will change its sound, and that implies there are certain situations where the sound will indeed change, so what are these situations?

## The letter 'Y'

The letter Y appears frequently in Welsh words, as it is a vowel in our language. Even in the Welsh version of the term *'The Mabinogi'*, you will see that it becomes *'Y Mabinogi'*. In this context the letter Y is actually a full word! It translates to mean 'the'. In *'Y Mabinogi'* the Y is pronounced 'uh', similar to how the letter U sounds in English words such as sun, fun, or turn.

However, the letter Y is a complicated letter in Welsh, as it is the only letter which really changes its sound depending on context. For example, the word *Ysbyty* (hospital) has three Y's, the first two Ys are pronounced as I explained above, with an 'uh' sound. The third Y, however, is pronounced a tad differently. There is no English equivalent to explain how it is pronounced here, the closest is that it sounds similar to the sound a double E makes in words such as bee, or tree.

The Y only changes to make the 'ee' sound in certain words, predominantly multi-syllabic words with multiple Y's, and also when a circumflex can be found above the Y as such: ŷ.

## The Circumflex, or 'Little Roof'

Another occasion where letters will change in their pronunciation is when a circumflex is present. In Welsh we refer to the circumflex as a *'To Bach'* which translates literally to mean a 'little roof'. Because that is exactly what it looks like, a little roof above the letters. You will find a circumflex above vowels in certain words.

A rather tired and uneducated joke about the Welsh language is that we supposedly have no vowels. This isn't true, the reason English speakers may believe this is because we have a different set of vowels to the English language. Our vowels are as follows:

A Guide to Welsh Pronunciation

a, e, i, o, u, w, y

Technically, we have more vowels than English! And each vowel is pronounced as such:

A = 'ah', as in 'Apple'.

E = as in the 'e' in 'bed', never as in 'be'.

I = 'ee', as in the double ee in 'tree'.

O = 'Aw', as in the 'O' in 'From'.

U = A slightly difficult one for non-Welsh speakers. Essentially an 'ee' noise, as in 'tree', but with the tongue rolled into the shape of a 'U'.

W – 'ooh', as in the noise the double o makes in 'Food'.

Y – As mentioned earlier, this is one of the only Welsh letters which can change depending on context. For the most part 'Y' is pronounced 'Uh', as in the sound U makes in English in words such as 'turn', or like the noise e makes in words such as 'The'. However, sometimes, usually in multi-syllabic words, the Y becomes more of an 'ee' sound, more or less indistinguishable from the Welsh 'U'. The best word to showcase this difference in pronunciation is 'Ysbyty', the Welsh word for 'hospital', which has three Ys. The first two Ys are pronounced as 'Uh', whereas the final Y is pronounced more so as an ee noise. Uss-BUTT-ee.

When the vowels have a circumflex above them, they will look like this:

â, ê, î, ô, û, ŵ, ŷ

The purpose of the circumflex is to extend the sound of the letter. So, for example, an A goes from being an 'ah' to a longer, more pronounced 'aah'. This is a difficult concept to explain in writing, and therefore I suggest looking to my YouTube videos for further clarity.

Over on my YouTube channel I already have several videos which go through the pronunciation of names, and words featured in Welsh myth and lore. You can find me under the username 'Mhara Starling'.

## Double Letters

Another fairly daunting aspect of the Welsh language may be the appearance of seemingly 'double letter' letters in our alphabet. These are as follows:

ch, dd, ff, ng, ll, ph, rh, and th

To those whose first language is English, it may seem strange to consider what appears to be two letters together as one singular letter. However, individual letters they are. Each of these letters create a specific sound as follows:

ch – A throaty sound, emanating from the back of the throat. Similar to how a Scottish person would pronounce the ch in Loch. It is not an S sound, nor a sound similar to the ch in English words such as Cheek.

dd – The sound of this letter comes from the front of the mouth. Similar to the sound of th in English words such as there, them and this but not like the th sound in English words such as thick or thin.

ff – This is a hard F sound as in the English words fight, freedom or full. The singular F in Welsh is a V noise as in video.

# A Guide to Welsh Pronunciation

ng – Thing of ng as the same sound found at the end of English words such as thinking, listening, or singing.

ll – The double L letter is one of the most complex Welsh letters. There is no English counterpart. It is a sound similar to that of a hiss.

ph – Simply pronounced similarly to the ph in the English word phrase.

rh – Very similar to a rolling R sound when used within words. Roll your R and then exhale or sigh while doing so.

th – Pronounced as the th in the English words thick, and thin.

In the glossary below I will not list the sounds these letters make in the names, I will instead include these letters as they are, please refer to the guide above for the pronunciation of said letters.

# Glossary of Names

Here I have provided a list of several characters and locations mentioned in this book, and detailed how to pronounce their names. For further guidance, look to my YouTube channel as stated above to hear the names sounded out.

**Annwfn (Ann-OO-vuhn)** – Also spelled Annwn (ANN-oon). The Welsh Otherworld.

**Arawn (AR-ow-n)** – Lord of Annwfn, the Otherworld, in the first branch of the *Mabinogi*.

**Arianrhod/Aranrhod (Ah-ree-ANN-rod/Ah-RAN-rod)** – From the fourth branch of the *Mabinogi*, sister of Gwydion.

**Awen (AH-when)** – Blessed, holy gift of inspiration. A force that flows from the Otherworld like a river or a gentle breeze, and we make form of it.

**Blodeuedd (Blaw-DAY-edd)** – A woman conjured from flowers in the fourth branch of the *Mabinogi*. She was made purely to be a wife to Lleu Llaw Gyffes (Llay llOW Guff-ess) and when she attempted to murder Lleu she was transformed into an Owl by Gwydion, and thus became Blodeuwedd (Blaw-DAY-whedd).

**Brân (Br-AH-n)** – A giant and King of Wales in the second branch of the *Mabinogi*. Also known by the epithet Bendigeidfran (Ben-dee-GAYD-vrahn) meaning Brân the blessed.

**Branwen (BRAHN-when)** – Brân's sister, who was married to the Irish king in the second branch of the *Mabinogi*. The abuse she suffered under the hand of the Irish caused a war between the Irish and the Welsh.

**Cerridwen (Kerr-ID-when)** – Witch, Goddess, and Mother. She who brewed a potion of pure Awen in order to help her son overcome his utter ugliness.

**Cŵn Annwn/Annwfn (COON ANN-oon/Ann-OO-vn)** – The hounds of the Otherworld, beings that have pure white fur everywhere on their bodies except their ears, which are blood red.

**Dyfed (DUH-ved)** – In Welsh history, a region in the South-West of Wales. In mythology, the Kingdom ruled over by Pwyll, who went on to marry Rhiannon.

**Dylan (Duh-LANN)** – A boy birthed from Aranrhod after she stepped over Math's magic wand. He took on the nature of the sea.

**Gorsedd Arberth (Gorr-SETH Arr-BEAR-th)** – A significant hill in Welsh mythology where Pwyll sees Rhiannon from for the first time.

**Gwydion (Gwee-dee-ONN)** – A mischievous magician from the fourth branch of the *Mabinogi*.

**Hafgan (Hav-GANN)** – A King in the Otherworld who fights with Arawn.

**Lleu Llaw Gyffes (*Ll*-ay *Ll*-OW Guff-ESS)** – Light of skilful hand, the rejected son of Aranrhod, who married Blodeuedd in the fourth branch.

**Llwyd ap Cilcoed (LlOO-id app Kill-COYED)** – A character in the third branch of the *Mabinogi* who is likely Otherworldly in nature.

**Mabinogi (Mabb-ee-NOGG-ee)** – The four branches of the *Mabinogi* make up what is considered the primary corpus of Welsh mythology.

**Manawydan (Mahn-ah-WID-ann)** – Son of Llŷr, second consort of Rhiannon, and one of the seven survivors of the war in the second branch.

**Math (Mah-*th*)** – Magician King of Gwynedd in the fourth branch. His name is pronounced exactly as you would pronounce the 'math' in 'mathematics'.

**Pryderi (PrUH-deh-ree)** – The son of Pwyll and Rhiannon, the only character present in all four branches of the *Mabinogi*.

**Pwyll (PWEE-ll)** – The prince of Dyfed, and later named the chief of the Otherworld in the first branch of the *Mabinogi*.

**Rhiannon (Rhee-ANN-onn)** – An Otherworldly character who marries Pwyll, prince of Dyfed and later Manawydan, son of Llŷr.

**Ynys Gwales (UHN-iss Goo-AL-ess)** – An island which in Welsh mythology was a place where time, and grief had no effect on those upon the island.

**Yr Hen Ogledd (Uhrr HEHNN OGG-laydd)** – "The old North", a term applied to a once Brythonic region in the Southernmost part of Scotland, and Northernmost part of England.

# Bibliography

Bollard, J. K. (1983). *The role of myth and tradition in the Four Branches of the Mabinogi.* Cambridge Medieval Celtic Studies Warwickshire, (6), 67-86.

Bollard, J. K. (2020*). The Structure of the Four Branches of the Mabinogi.* In *The Mabinogi (Routledge Revivals),* (pp. 165-196). Routledge.

Breeze, A. (2009). *The origins of the Four Branches of the Mabinogi.* Gracewing.

Bromwich, R. (2020). *The Mabinogion and Lady Charlotte Guest.* In *The Mabinogi (Routledge Revivals),* (pp. 3-18). Routledge.

Bromwich, R. (Ed.). (2014). *Trioedd Ynys Prydein: The Triads of the Island of Britain.* University of Wales Press.

Charles-Edwards, T. M. (2020). *The Date of the Four Branches of the Mabinogi.* In *The Mabinogi (Routledge Revivals),* (pp. 19-58). Routledge.

Coileáin, S. Ó. (1977). *A Thematic Study of the Tale "Pwyll Pendeuic Dyuet".* Studia Celtica, 12, 78.

Davies, S. (1989). *Pedeir Keinc y Mabinogi.* Gomer Press.

Davies, Sioned. (Ed.). (2007). *The Mabinogion.* Oxford University Press, USA.

Elsbeth, M. & Johnson, K. (1997). *The Silver Wheel: Women's Myths and Mysteries in the Celtic Tradition.* Llewellyn Worldwide.

Farrar, J. & Farrar, S. (1987). *The Witches' Goddess: The Feminine Principle of Divinity.* Robert Hale.

Ford, P. K. (1981). *Prolegomena to a Reading of the Mabinogi: 'Pwyll' and 'Manawydan'.* Studia Celtica, 16, 110.

Ford, P. K. (1987). Branwen: a study of the Celtic affinities. Studia Celtica, 22, 29.

Ford, Patrick. K. (1977). trans. *The Mabinogi and Other Medieval Welsh Tales.* University of California Press.

Gardner, G. B. (1959). *The Meaning of Witchcraft*. The Aquarian Press, London.

Graves, R. (1948). *The White Goddess*. Faber and Faber Ltd. London. Reprint, (1999).

Gruffydd, W. J. (1953). *Rhiannon: An Inquiry into the Origin of the First and Third Branches of the Mabinogi*. Cardiff: University of Wales Press.

Hanson-Smith, E. (2020). *Pwyll Prince of Dyfed: the narrative structure*. In *The Mabinogi (Routledge Revivals)*, (pp. 153-164). Routledge.

Haycock, M. (2007). *Legendary poems from the Book of Taliesin*. CMCS publications.

Hughes, K. (2014). *The Book of Celtic Magic: Transformative Teachings from the Cauldron of Awen*. Llewellyn Worldwide.

Hughes, Kristoffer. (2021). *Cerridwen: Celtic Goddess of Inspiration*. Llewellyn Worldwide.

Hutton, R. (2023, April 26th). *Finding Lost Gods in Wales*. Gresham College. file:///C:/Users/mhara/Downloads/2023-04-26-1800_Hutton-T%20(1).pdf [Accessed: December 23rd, 2023].

Ifans, D. & Ifans, R. (2007). *Y Mabinogion*. Gwasg Gomer, Ceredigion.

Jones, T. G. (1930). *Welsh Folklore and Folk Custom*. Reprint, Cockatrice Books (2020).

Keefer, S. L. (1989). *The Lost Tale of Dylan in the Fourth Branch of the "Mabinogi"*. Studia Celtica, 24, 26.

McKenna, C. A. (2020). *The Theme of Sovereignty in Pwyll*. In *The Mabinogi (Routledge Revivals)*, (pp. 303-330). Routledge.

Rodway, S. (2018). *The Mabinogi and the shadow of Celtic mythology*. Studia Celtica, 52(1), 67-85.

Rudiger, A. (2022). *Y Tylwyth Teg. an Analysis of a Literary Motif*. Bangor University (United Kingdom).

Shack, J. (2015, January). *Otherworld and Norman 'Other': Annwfn and its colonial implications in the First Branch of the Mabinogi*. In *Proceedings of the Harvard Celtic colloquium* (pp. 172-186).

The Department of Celtic Languages and Literatures Faculty of Arts and Sciences, Harvard University.

Sims-Williams, P. (2011). *Irish influence on medieval Welsh literature*. Oxford University Press.

Sullivan, C. W. (2020). *Inheritance and lordship in Math*. In *The Mabinogi (Routledge Revivals)*, (pp. 347-366). Routledge.

Sullivan, C. W. (Ed.). (1996). *The Mabinogi: A Book of Essays* (Vol. 16). Psychology Press.

Thomas, W. J. (1907). *The Welsh Fairy Book*. TF Unwin. (Facsimile Copy).

Valente, R. L. (2020). *Gwydion and Aranrhod: crossing the borders of gender in Math*. In *The Mabinogi (Routledge Revivals)*, (pp. 331-345). Routledge.

Welsh, A. (2020). *Manawydan fab Llŷr: Wales, England, and the "New Man"*. In *The Mabinogi (Routledge Revivals)* (pp. 121-141). Routledge.

Welsh, A. (2020). *Manawydan fab Llŷr: Wales, England, and the "New Man"*. In *The Mabinogi (Routledge Revivals)* (pp. 121-141). Routledge.

Williams, I. (1930). *Pedeir Keinc Y Mabinogi*. Gwasg Prifysgol Cymru, Cardiff.

Wood, J. (1985). *The calumniated wife in medieval Welsh literature*. Cambridge medieval Celtic studies, 10, pp. 25-38.

# MOON BOOKS

## PAGANISM & SHAMANISM

What is Paganism? A religion, a spirituality, an alternative belief system, nature worship? You can fi nd support for all these definitions (and many more) in dictionaries, encyclopaedias, and text books of religion, but subscribe to any one and the truth will evade you. Above all Paganism is a creative pursuit, an encounter with reality, an exploration of meaning and an expression of the soul. Druids, Heathens, Wiccans and others, all contribute their insights and literary riches to the Pagan tradition. Moon Books invites you to begin or to deepen your own encounter, right here, right now.

If you have enjoyed this book, why not tell other readers by posting a review on your preferred book site.

# Bestsellers from Moon Books

## Pagan Portals Series
## The Morrigan
Meeting the Great Queens
Morgan Daimler
*Ancient and enigmatic, the Morrigan reaches out to us.*
*On shadowed wings and in raven's call, meet the ancient Irish*
*goddess of war, battle, prophecy, death, sovereignty, and magic.*
Paperback: 978-1-78279-833-0 ebook: 978-1-78279-834-7

## The Awen Alone
Walking the Path of the Solitary Druid
Joanna van der Hoeven
*An introductory guide for the solitary Druid, The Awen Alone will*
*accompany you as you explore, and seek out your own place*
*within the natural world.*
Paperback: 978-1-78279-547-6 ebook: 978-1-78279-546-9

## Moon Magic
Rachel Patterson
*An introduction to working with the phases of the Moon,*
*what they are and how to live in harmony with the lunar*
*year and to utilise all the magical powers it provides.*
Paperback: 978-1-78279-281-9 ebook: 978-1-78279-282-6

## Hekate
A Devotional
Vivienne Moss
*Hekate, Queen of Witches and the Shadow-Lands,*
*haunts the pages of this devotional bringing magic*
*and enchantment into your lives.*
Paperback: 978-1-78535-161-7 ebook: 978-1-78535-162-4

## Bestsellers from Moon Books

### Keeping Her Keys
An Introduction to Hekate's Modern Witchcraft
Cyndi Brannen
*Blending Hekate, witchcraft and personal development together to create a powerful new magickal perspective.*
Paperback: 978-1-78904-075-3 ebook 978-1-78904-076-0

### Journey to the Dark Goddess
How to Return to Your Soul
Jane Meredith
*Discover the powerful secrets of the Dark Goddess and transform your depression, grief and pain into healing and integration.*
Paperback: 978-1-84694-677-6 ebook: 978-1-78099-223-5

### Shamanic Reiki
Expanded Ways of Working with Universal Life Force Energy
Llyn Roberts, Robert Levy
*Shamanism and Reiki are each powerful ways of healing; together, their power multiplies. Shamanic Reiki introduces techniques to help healers and Reiki practitioners tap ancient healing wisdom.*
Paperback: 978-1-84694-037-8 ebook: 978-1-84694-650-9

### Southern Cunning
Folkloric Witchcraft in the American South
Aaron Oberon
*Modern witchcraft with a Southern flair, this book is a journey through the folklore of the American South and a look at the power these stories hold for modern witches.*
Paperback: 978-1-78904-196-5 ebook: 978-1-78904-197-2

Readers of ebooks can buy or view any of these bestsellers by clicking on the live link in the title. Most titles are published in paperback and as an ebook. Paperbacks are available in traditional bookshops. Both print and ebook formats are available online.

Find more titles and sign up to our readers' newsletter
http://www.johnhuntpublishing.com/paganism

For video content, author interviews and more, please subscribe to our YouTube channel.

## MoonBooksPublishing

Follow us on social media for book news, promotions and more:

## Facebook: Moon Books

## Instagram: @MoonBooksCI

## X: @MoonBooksCI

## TikTok: @MoonBooksCI